GOD'S ENDTIME ARMY

Terry L. Ball

CONTENTS

FOREWORD

It is with great joy and humility that I have the honor to write the foreword for this remarkable book *God's Endtime Army* penned by my dear friend and fellow minister of the gospel Apostle Terry Ball. For over three decades, he has faithfully served God's people with unwavering dedication, profound wisdom, and deep love for the Lord Jesus Christ.

Throughout his ministry, I have witnessed first-hand the prophetic insights and spiritual depth that flow from his heart. His words are not mere rhetoric but a powerful manifestation of God's grace working through him to touch lives, transform hearts, and bring hope to those in need.

In these pages, you will find a treasure trove of spiritual truths, practical wisdom, and heartfelt reflections that will inspire you to draw closer to God and deepen your faith journey. As you delve into this book, may you be blessed abundantly by the words written with such grace and anointing by my dear friend.

I wholeheartedly recommend this book as a valuable resource for all seeking spiritual growth, deeper understanding of God's word, and a closer walk with our Savior. May it ignite a flame within your soul to pursue God wholeheartedly and experience His transformative power in your life. May this book serve as a beacon of light in a world filled with darkness, guiding you towards a deeper relationship with our Lord Jesus Christ. Let its pages be a source of inspiration, encouragement, and enlightenment on your journey of faith.

With gratitude for his friendship and admiration for his ministry,

Bishop John Jackson, D.D.
Greater Works Global CDC

PREFACE

Prophet Terry Ball:
A Vessel of God's Message

The Lord has truly been using this anointed vessel in a remarkable and special way. God has used him to touch the lives of many, especially our leaders. Through his ministry, Prophet Terry Ball has become a beacon of deep spirituality; He has brought hope and inspiration to countless believers.

In these times of uncertainty and spiritual warfare, it is crucial that we heed the words spoken through Prophet Terry Ball. His messages are not mere words but divine revelations that resonate with the truth of God's Word. As Apostle Johnny L. Kemp rightly points out, we are living in an hour of deception and apostasy: where the enemy seeks to lead astray. The elect of God have become the enemy's target of deception. It is therefore imperative that we pay attention to the prophetic insights shared by Prophet Terry Ball.

Prophet Terry Ball's alignment with the end time message for the body of Christ is a testament to his obedience to God's calling. As you open your hearts and minds to receive his teachings, I am confident that you will be transformed and renewed in your faith journey. Let us not overlook this appointed time for spiritual growth and enlightenment.

May we all draw closer to God through the ministry of Prophet Terry Ball, allowing his words to guide us in these challenging times. Together, let us stand firm in our faith and embrace the prophetic wisdom being imparted through this chosen vessel.

Apostle Johnny L. Kemp
CEO, MEC Ministries Inc.
Miami, FL

1
GOD'S SPECIAL FORCES

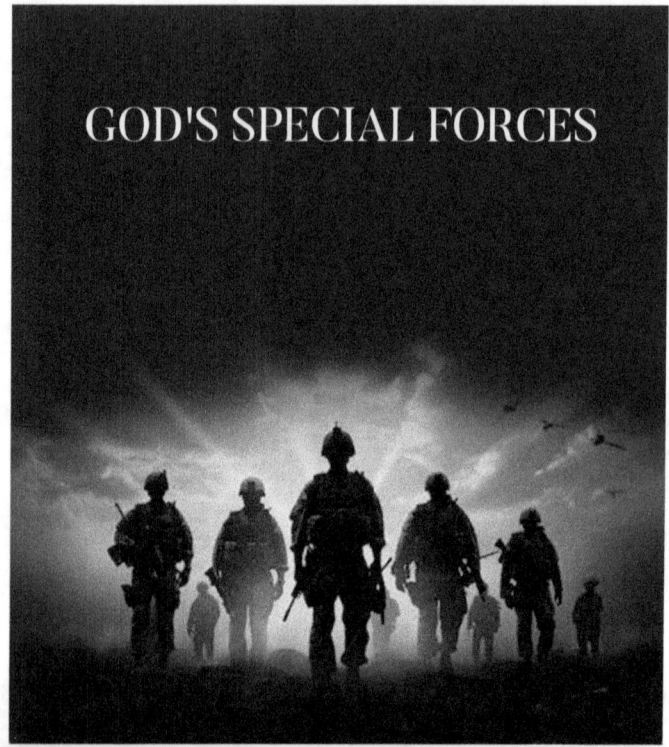

GOD'S SPECIAL FORCES

1 Chronicles 7:11
All these the sons of Jediael, by the heads of their fathers,
mighty men of valour, were seventeen thousand and
two hundred soldiers, fit to go out
for war and battle.

Welcome to all my readers!

God's Endtime Army is *not* just another book. It is a prophetic revelation of God's end-time army and what God is doing in the body of Christ with *His* end-time warriors. We are living in a two-fold time of catastrophic and fascinating happenings. There is the house of David, and there is the house of Saul, and they exist simultaneously.

Throughout the body of Christ, you have heard the phrase, "No more church as usual". That is not just a phrase—it is a revelation! Something in the Church has to change! The mindset of those who go to church has to change! Yes, indeed!

Later, we will jump into 1 Chronicles chapter twelve to see how God, by His Spirit, is summoning His **ELITE.** We must understand that the heart of God in past times remains the same today. Historically, one of the main emphases of 1 and 2 Chronicles centers around rebuilding the Temple. God does not need a temple; he needs a people willing to take a stand for his word. He needs a people who are not just churchgoers but kingdom citizens who are doers of the word. Over time, true believers develop a passion and a hunger for more extraordinary things of God. These are the candidates for God's Endtime Army.

Let's take a historical glance at 1 Chronicles, chapters ten and eleven, which will help us understand chapter twelve. In chapter ten, we see the tragic end to the reign of King Saul. Saul did many things wrong, but the greatest was that, as King, *he never pursued the presence of God.* There is a significant shift in ministry as we know it: a move from performance to presence ministry. Only because of God's grace will we continue to see the Saul-type ministry; however, with slight effectiveness. An example of this is depicted in 1 Samuel 18:7 when Saul and David's ministries were compared. We learn that, "**Saul has killed his thousands, and David his ten thousands!**" (1 Samuel 18:7). The David-type ministry will demonstrate powerful Endtime movements of God.

In chapter eleven, we see David being anointed King and taking on the role of a **WARRIOR KING.** Wow! It is so prophetically awesome! His title as King never moved him. He led his people into many battles. I'm sure you all remember the old saying, "I can show you better than I can tell you!". That is how David reigned as King.

The Kingdom Is Summoning The Elite

¹ Now these are they that came to David to Ziklag, while he yet kept himself close because of Saul the son of Kish: ² They were armed with bows and could use both the right hand and the left in hurling stones and shooting arrows out of a bow, even of Saul's brethren of Benjamin. ⁸ And of the Gadites there separated themselves unto David into the hold to the wilderness men of might, and men of war fit for the battle, that could handle shield and buckler, whose faces were like the faces of lions, and were as swift as the roes upon the mountains. and they were among the mighty men, helpers of the war.

1 Chronicles 12:1-2,8 KJV

You have just read an account of David, a man of war. He is in the midst of a significant transition and transformation at the same time. His life story speaks prophetically to anyone ready to answer the call of God and move from a church mindset to a kingdom army mindset.

Wow, I love the opening sentence of 1 Chronicles 12:1, " **and these are they that came to David at**

Ziklag". As we examine this verse, we see how the mighty men of war responded to David. They most likely admired his courageous leadership qualities, which became evident when he made a hallmark statement before the Israeli army, "**Is there not a cause?**" (1 Samuel 17:29). David was still a youth but ready to confront his nation's worst enemy, the mighty warrior Goliath.

Today, you may be in a similar place: on the backside of the desert. It feels like no one knows your name, and no one knows who you are. This is a critical season to strengthen your character and integrity. That is how it all began for David, who was not yet reigning as King. For many of you reading this book, this chapter will draw out a prophetic moment in your life. It is giving you revelation, impartation, and activation for your season as a person of WAR. Not only was David a man of war, but God surrounded him with mighty warriors. Biblical history correctly shows us David's army winning battle after battle. **I declare and decree, so shall it be with you!**

The Spirit of the Lord is prophetically calling the remnant, God's Endtime Army, to the front of the line. You may ask, "Why?". My response has a binary meaning. On the one side, there is a great storm coming to the earth, and at the same time, a great revival is on the spiritual horizon. The word of God calls this great revival the latter and the former rain of God, also known as *The Outpouring*. Yes, start preparing for another tremendous outpouring. We are going to experience something more than what we have ever known!

God's consecrated vessels, those on the back side of the desert, are being summoned to *SHIFT.* You must step from your NOW to your NEXT! The SHIFT is for the no-names, those without mega-churches, and those who may be unknown in ministry circles. Despite your perceived status, you have authority with God and heaven.

Scripture teaches us that demons do not respect who you are but whose you are, "But the wicked spirit, answering, said to them: "Jesus I know, and Paul I know; but who are you?". Unfortunately, many churchgoers are unknown in heaven because the Church has been going through its pandemic. The Apostle Peter lets us know that God does not show favoritism or partiality, "**Then Peter opened his mouth, and said, of a truth I perceive that God is no respecter of persons: But in every nation, he that feareth him, and worketh righteousness, is accepted with him**" (Acts 10:34-35). That was David's story. His family overlooked him during battle and when the Prophet Samuel came to anoint the next King of Israel. They were too familiar with him and did not see him as kingly or mighty and courageous—their pride and prejudice prevented them from seeing God's ultimate purpose.

Jehovah-Nissi[1] is one of the great names of our Father God: the Lord God of battle. He is already summoning and assembling His Army to battle. It is time to prepare for war! This is not a war that we have not won through Christ Jesus, but we must show up to the battle with our faith and say, like David, "Is there not a cause?". In times of war or uncertainty, a special breed of warrior is ready to answer its nation's call. Just like in the regular army, a battle begins before a battle begins. What do I mean by that? History will tell you that there was a battle before World War One, World War 2, the Vietnam War, or even the recent wars that have started. The Army, the Navy, and the Marine Corps send their special forces in first, *The Elite Ones*. They are the ones to go in first, not to fight the entire war. These Special Forces are unique because they work in peacetime, conflict, and war, implementing unconventional air, land, or sea operations. They engage in direct action missions and

---

1. **YAHWEH-NISSI [*yah*-way-nee-*see*]**: "The Lord Our Banner" (Exodus 17:15), where *the banner* is understood to be a rallying place. This name commemorates the desert victory over the Amalekites in Exodus 17. (Bible Study Tools)

reconnaissance missions around the world. They extract high-level officials captured by the enemy. Most of all, they extract Intel and the enemy's secrets and activities. The Elites also go first to pioneer the ground and to lay the foundation for battle. Their missions include offensive raids, demolitions, surveillance, search and rescue, and counterterrorism. The Elites establish the initial confrontation with the enemy to let them know they are coming to take their territory back.

I can show you a list of old covenant Elite Warriors like Moses, Joshua, and Caleb, as well as judges named in the book of Judges like Deborah and Samson. Several Old Testament Prophets like Samuel, Elijah, and Ezekiel are among countless Elites. The distinguishing thing about them was their exceptional life of consecration and separation unto God. We have two men on this list who fasted forty days and forty nights: Moses and Elijah. They were seen in person in the New Testament during Jesus' Transfiguration on the mount because of their commitment to consecration in the latter part of their lives. That is a little deep for some!

Looking back over the last 100 years, I can give you name after name of people who consecrated themselves to God and became candidates for the remnant army of their era—names like William J Seymour, Franklin Hall, William Branham, TL Osborn, and A. A. Allen. I encourage you, especially my new younger listeners, to study the lives of these patriots from the last move of God in the previous 100 years. I apologize for not having the opportunity to name countless others. Take time to research and study them, and you will discover they were Elite. You will be amazed at how God moved through their lives and demonstrated His miraculous power.

Let me say this to all who are in the ministry of the Gospel of Jesus Christ: we must be hungry for *His presence*, not the pulpit. Showmanship comes in speech articulation, but it will not get it done on this elite level.

[14]For many are called, but few are chosen.

Matthew 22:14 KJV

A Famous Quote
"If you build an army of 100 lions and their leader is a dog, in any fight, the lions will die like a dog. But if you build an army of 100 dogs and their leader is a lion, all dogs will fight as a lion."

Napolean

A New Wineskin For A New Season
 37 And no one pours new wine into
old wineskins; if he does, the fresh
wine will burst the skins and it will be
spilled and the skins will be ruined (destroyed). 38 But new wine must be put
into fresh wineskins.

Luke 5:37-38 AMPC

Now, my friend, let us investigate the word *new*.
Before we examine the phrase wineskin in context
of God's seasons, we must first recognize that the
Father is always endeavoring to do something new.
This is mentioned in various places in Scripture.
2 Corinthians 5:17 says, "**Therefore if any man
be in Christ, he is a new creature: old things
are passed away; behold, all things are become new**". Isaiah 43:19a states, "**Behold, I will
do a new thing; now it shall spring forth; shall
ye not know it?**". Colossians 3:10 instructs us to,
"**Put on your new nature, and be renewed as
you learn to know your Creator and become
like him**". Revelation 21:5 records, "**And he that
sat upon the throne said, Behold, I make all
things new. And he said unto me, Write: for
these words are true and faithful**". AMEN!!
You will understand my point of reference if you
do a word study. God is doing a new thing among

His people! The entire purpose of the new wineskin is to prepare the Church, God's bride, for the
final battle and coming of our Lord Jesus Christ.
Many hear the Holy Spirit's beckoning, so they are
stretched from the old wineskin mindset to walk
in the Spirit. I refer to this as the *Gethsemane Encounter.* As you read below, you will see that our
Lord and Savior, Jesus Christ, had to go through
Gethsemane: a place of pressure and pressing oil
(or wine). Those two terminologies describe what
Gethsemane means. It took stretching Jesus' earthly
will to die so that He could fulfill His Kingdom
assignment.

> [36] Then cometh Jesus with them unto
> a place called Gethsemane, and saith
> unto the disciples, Sit ye here, while I
> go and pray yonder. [37] And he took with
> him Peter and the two sons of Zebedee,
> and began to be sorrowful and very
> heavy. [38] Then saith he unto them, My
> soul is exceeding sorrowful, even unto
> death: tarry ye here, and watch with
> me.
>
> Matthew 26:36-38 KJV

My book may not become a New York Times
bestseller. Who knows? Maybe it will! Regardless,
I desire to reach Soldiers in the Lord's Army. I

want to encourage them to press on and embrace the revelation. If you can gasp this calling of the new wineskin, you will soon find yourself in a new season of life. Press on, my brother! Press on, my sister!

Let us look at the new wineskin prophetically before we conclude the subject. Jesus had twelve disciples. He only asked three of them to go a little further, to go to the next level, and make it to the next dimension. That is symbolic of the *Remnant Army*. As you go chapter by chapter into this book, you will understand that everybody is not going where you want to get to in God. Many will stay in the "bless me" club: the level one saints who are merely churchy; however, Kingdom citizens will go after God with all their hearts! The Holy Spirit will enlist these candidates into God's Endtime Army.

This season, the Holy Ghost summons a Davidic Company of believers to accept the call and authority as God's Special Forces and to declare WAR! I want to share something compelling about David with you right now. David had a consecration toward worship. Most believers who do not have a consecration to define them in Christ need to begin to pursue one and acknowledge that God is calling them to live a consecrated life. Hear by the Spirit the words of our Lord Jesus Christ...."New Wine *MUST BE* put into new bottles/vessels."

Let us discuss one of the qualifications for becoming an Elite in the kingdom. If your strength is prayer, fasting, or worship like David, that discipline becomes your tool of consecration and the building block of your spiritual strength. David's worship on the backside of the desert offers two statements that are the proper terminology for consecration: The crucified life or dying to self. Wow, hit up one of the social media platforms quickly, and tell me when you last heard one of those heart-wrenching messages. What is the relevance of fasting, praying, or worshipping to becoming an elite Holy Ghost Navy Seal? Remember, the weapons of our warfare are not carnal or, should I say, natural?

The Gathering of
His Consecrated Vessels
5Gather my saint together onto me;
those that have made a covenant by
sacrifice.
Psalm 50:5 KJV

Our scripture confirms this very well through the Psalmist in Psalms 50. The scripture listed above is a Prophetic word for this season. The Jews have three significant feasts: Passover, Pentecost, and Tabernacles. Reflecting on these feasts helps me to understand that the Lord is raising a time of Tabernacling. There is a Holy Ghost net over the body of Christ, and a gathering is taking place. *The Tabernacle Effect* is the Endtime Army coming together.

Human beings are not orchestrating the gathering of the saints together. It is not traditions or doctrines of religion. This clarion call is to God's consecrated vessels. They know who they are, and they are discerning the sound from heaven. Like the Joshua generation, they are a generation that will obey. From this gathered company, we will come forward as different people, unlike what we have seen in the past. It will be the next level of ministry. It will not be about me and my ministry but Jesus Christ and His will.

His consecrated ones are on the earth, so make no mistake. My friend, God has an army. Yes, a people prepared for battle! They have been fasting and praying for many years now. There is a group of people who will be coming forward. They will come from the back side of the mountain, so to speak. They are gifted, anointed, and on fire for their God. I say this with prophetic confidence because I am one of them. These types of vessels are not in the ministry for showmanship. They are sold out to God and on another level. They bear the marks of a consecrated life. They carry the testimony of Christ Jesus as a badge of honor. Galatians 2:20 makes it simple; "**I am crucified with Christ; nevertheless, I live; yet not I, but Christ liveth in me: and the life which I now live in the flesh I live by the faith of the Son of God, who loved me, and gave himself for me**". These truly consecrated vessels speak about another in the ministry. They have entered into the priesthood. And they have revelation about who they are in the kingdom!

I am addressing this first letter to the remnant because there is a generation of people I call *Cruise Ship Saints.* The cruise ship saints are in it for the ride! They scream, "Give me my blessing, give me my prophecy, and give me this and that. Please don't ask me to do anything or to give anything because you know I'm easily offended!"

I always say, "God always has His people." I call them the army. They are the remnant. The consecrated ones are a slight majority of the body of Christ. I am writing this chapter for you: God's End-time Army. There is the Davidic company of saints, whom I call the *Battleship Saints*. Read the definition below of the place called Ziklag, where David and his mighty men met.

Yes, there are many at their place called Ziklag: the place of equipping and preparation in consecration. Ziklag has two meanings: the place of pouring and the place of the press or, should we say, the pressure[2] . David had his own weapons factory in Ziklag that is breaking the enemy's hold on blacksmiths. This weapons factor trains blacksmiths. It also designs, builds, and tests new weapons. David restored an empty place in the kingdom infrastructure that had put Israel in weakness with her enemies. While living in exile and running from Saul, God positioned David in Ziklag so he could become the strongest King in the nation's history! David became a supplier of the very thing the enemy sought to limit! Ziklag was strategic for David. He ended up coming to the throne with his army and wealth. He restored the infrastructure of the kingdom.

In St. John chapter 14, Jesus said "**I go to prepare a place for you**", my remnant army (John 14:2). Make sure you are in the right place and have the right prophetic connections. There is a call to break off from the old and step into the new. Surrender your mindset so you can align with the new army you just joined. You must change how you think so you can become a warrior for a cause. Do you remember what David said when talking to King Saul and his entire army, who were afraid to go out and face the Goliath of their day? He asked them, "Is there not a cause?". If we were to answer

---

2. Ziklag is composed of two ancient Hebrew words that mean "to pour" and "to press." In other words, **Ziklag is a blacksmith center!**

that question today, the response is an absolute yes! There are many causes why we need to hear this summoning call of the Holy Spirit to prepare for battle.

> [1] Now the Philistines gathered together their armies to battle and were gathered together at Shochoh, which belongeth to Judah and pitched between Shochoh and Azekah, in Ephesdammim. [2] And Saul and the men of Israel were gathered together, and pitched by the valley of Elah, and set the battle in array against the Philistines.
>
> 1 Samuel 17:1-2 KJV

Look at this outstanding example of the two armies being summoned to battle. First, we have the enemy in verse one, the Philistine, who comes to war ready to fight. They pulled out their special forces unit on Israel. They left King Saul shocked! When Goliath came out to battle on behalf of the Philistines, no one in the army of Israel wanted to battle. A similar trend is happening with the enemies attacking us now. I see the same thing with today's Church. Verse two informs us that their cells were set in the battle array. This means that they looked the part; it was sharp now. They were dressed with their armor and weapons of war. The only thing they were lacking was the heart to fight. Yes, we go to Church, get decked out, get dressed up, and all of that. We have the sermons, listen to the choir, and follow all of the prerequisites of a good Saint of God. However, we have never addressed the real issues: the spiritual realm, the Kingdom of Darkness, and the moral decay in our communities. We ignored the long list of homosexual issues, agenda issues, and more. We want to preach, prophesy, and perform, but we do not want to address the actual battle: the real Goliaths.

A Famous Quote
Shall I tell you why young men love war? In peace, there's a hundred questions with a thousand answers! In war, there's only one question with one right answer
Maria Doria Russell

Countless Old and New Testament men and women of God were summoned to battle as special forces in their day. They had to take a stand. Daniel did not bow despite being summoned to the world's court on several occasions. We have John the Baptist, who is willing to confront what was wrong in his day and take a stand. Of course, our Lord and Savior, Jesus Christ, addressed many issues when

He was summoned. Jesus came forth as the son of
man. He did not come with all His authority as the
Son of God. Instead, He laid that down. As the son
of man, He confronted many things in His three and
a half years of earthly ministry. John the Baptist and
Jesus were both committed to the Nazirite vows.
That is what I am saying about consecration. There
is a resounding call to a consecrated lifestyle. You
can agree that Jesus and John the Baptist can be
considered the special forces of their day.

Notice that in verse one of 1 Samuel 17, the
Philistines immediately responded to the call to
war. Do not forget that your adversary, the devil,
respects authority and nothing else, in Jesus' name.
Ephesians chapter 6 outlines four classifications or
levels of satanic power and rank (Ephesians 6:12).
Now, they want to set and control the atmosphere
and the climate of cities, towns, villages, and nations. The keyword is to govern city governance
over the people. That is why God gave man dominion through Adam in the very beginning. We call it
Kingdom Dominion. What we see happening with
King David is that God was setting him up to take
territory and dominion. That is what kings do!

What we see in 1 Chronicles chapter 12 is a summoning of the Elite to come and stand with those
Davids of today. Prophetically, this is what is happening. There is a call to the Elite in the kingdom,
the well-prepared, consecrated, soldiers of God, to

come into kingdom order and protocol. There is a mandate for them to have a keen understanding of their kingdom assignment.

Old Testament Types and Shadows

> ⁵ Who serve unto the example and shadow of heavenly things, as Moses was admonished of God when he was about to make the tabernacle: for, See, saith he, that thou make all things according to the pattern shewed to thee in the mount.
>
> Hebrews 8:5 KJV

> ³² And what shall I more say? for the time would fail me to tell of Gideon, and of Barak, and of Samson, and of Jephthae; of David also, and Samuel, and of the prophets: ³³ Who through faith subdued kingdoms, wrought righteousness, obtained promises, stopped the mouths of lions. ³⁴ Quenched the violence of fire, escaped the edge of the sword, out of weakness were made strong, waxed valiant in fight, turned to flight the armies of the aliens.³⁵ Women

received their dead raised to life again:
and others were tortured, not accepting
deliverance; that they might obtain a
better resurrection:

Hebrews 11:32-35 NKJV

Wow, can we say God's Special Forces, with a big
amen! After reading that eleventh chapter, if I were
a lawyer, I would say, "Judge, I rest my case". You
can write an entire book on that eleventh chapter
of the book of Hebrews. It is a phenomenal book
of Elite ones in the Kingdom of God. If you go
up a few verses in the eleventh chapter, you will
see where Bible characters known for their faith,
like Enoch, Noah, and Abraham, are more than
Bible characters; they are among the Elite. They
lived through circumstances and sought to obey
the heart of God. Their eliteness came about by
building altars unto God, sacrificing by consecrat-
ing themselves in prayer, and obeying His voice
consistently. For example, Abraham demonstrated
twenty-five years of walking through a faith journey. Noah's life represents 120 years of obedience.
You get my point! I want us to avoid getting caught
up in phenomenal life stories. Instead, I want you to
understand today, as you read this book, that God is
no respecter of persons. He is ready to demonstrate
his power and glory through your life.

Now, as we think about our New Testament Apostles who followed Jesus Christ and obtained personal, hands-on training with Him over three years, it is safe to say that they were elite and special forces. The Church of Antioch and the Jerusalem Church produced the apostles of the Book of Acts because of the persecution they endured in those days. They had their own Gethsemane experiences during that era. They have their winepress history. Their lives were on the line daily. I encourage you to read Foxes Book of Martyrs. What they went through produced some incredible early church apostles, known as apostolic fathers today.

Let Us Take A Look At Uncle Sam's Example: The United States Military

The United States of America has a military covering four different governmental protection branches. Within these four branches, I find the natural and spiritual parallels that describe the Army of the Lord [the Body of Christ]. Like in all military forces I have read about and researched, there is always an army within the army. That is where the term God's Special Forces originates from. Being a former Marine Corps veteran, I am familiar with regular and military special forces units. Regulars in the army are considered a soldier. Regulars in the navy are considered a sailor. The same goes for the Air Force and even the Marine Corps. Every soldier does not have the same passion as those who decided to become special forces. Note that being in the special forces is a *choice.* Anybody can join the military and become a soldier or a sailor. It is the same in the Church. People could join churches all the time. You can concur with what I'm saying: everyone in the Church does not have a passion for the things of God. The Bible is full of people who choose to be different, like Moses and Samuel. Throughout the Old Testament, we would have example after example.

Daniel is an excellent example. The Bible says he *purposed in his heart.* Daniel made a covenant with his heart, and because of that, he and the three Hebrew boys became elite in the Babylonian kingdom and Nebuchadnezzar court.

The United States Department of Defense classifies these groups as American Special Operations Forces. I know this is news to most of my readers, but as you can read below, there are countless Elite Forces within each military branch. Usually, when we think about the military, for instance, the army, we think about the primary army and a basic soldier. However, all military branches have what we call elite ones or special forces units. I encourage all of my readers to take one or two of these special forces units to do a little research. You will be amazed to learn the highly detailed and intricate years of training and preparation required to become one of these units. Regarding the Church and the believer, God also has his Elite soldiers. Some Elite Forces included:

- Army Green Berets

- Army Night Stalkers

- Army Rangers

- Navy SEALs

- Navy SEALs Missions

- Navy SWCCs

- Marine MARSOC

- Marine RECON

His Elites Ones

In this section about the Elite, I want to address some Old Testament typologies of the Elite. First, let me speak to my apostolic and prophetic community. Today, we should be leading the way as Apostles and Prophets. We should be known for our walk with God, prayer life, fasting life. We should be identified by the the signs, wonders, and miracles that follow our ministries. It is not enough to be recognized by title but we must be recognized by the authority from heaven that we walk in. That is what I call the Elite!

> [1] Now Peter and John went up together into the Temple at the hour of prayer, being the ninth hour. [2] And a certain man lame from his mother's womb was carried, whom they laid daily at the gate of the Temple which is called Beautiful, to ask alms of them that entered into the Temple; [3] Who seeing Peter and John about to go into the Temple asked for an alms. [4] And Peter, fastening his eyes upon him with John, said, Look on us.
>
> Acts 3:1-4 KJV

Now, this is what I'm talking about in Acts chapter 3; the earlier apostles were elite when it came to the power of God and walking in Kingdom authority. All believers today should make this their quest. The first Apostles set the bar very high, but we can reach it by executing the Commission and the more significant works that Jesus says we shall do (John 14:12). Look at this scripture: Acts chapter 3 in verse 4, says "**Look on us**". In this day and age, we must preach the same. We should not preach, "look at us." I must explain. We now commonly accept some things in ministry, such as, "How would you

homoletically construct a sermon?". Some believe it is essential to add jokes. Contrary to the
word of God, some choose to preach in a way
that does not make people feel uncomfortable in
their sin. There are two types of preachers today:
one group says, "Look at us," meaning watch me
perform, and the other says, "Look on us," as they
walk in God's authority and grace. When people
"looked upon Peter and the apostles," they saw
the authority of heaven. Peter consecrated his
life to God, and God honored his words. Instant-
ly, upon Peter's word, the man was healed.

Old Testament Elite Ones like Esther

For my sisters, there are many examples in
the word of God of female Elite ones. Let us
start with Queen Esther, who had to make a
life-or-death decision. Mordecai expressed that
God's purpose was paramount. She went in before the King and stood on behalf of her people.
Esther could have perished according to the law.
She had broken protocol. Elites sometimes have
to break protocol to do particular assignments to
fulfill the will of God on earth.

I could highlight several Old and New Testament
stories to show the journey of faith. But we now understand that many of the named Bible characters

are not regular people. They are people who did great kingdom exploits.

2

GOD'S ENDTIME ARMY

GOD'S ENDTIME ARMY

Joel 2:11
And the Lord shall utter his voice before his army:
for his camp is very great: for he is strong that
executeth his word: for the day of the
Lord is great and very terrible;
and who can abide it?

As we begin this chapter, I want to examine the title, God's End Time Army, to emphasize the name of the Lord our God. Jesus Christ's name is JEHO-VAH, meaning He is a man of war! It is essential to establish that fact because men and women in our churches have lost their fighting spirit. Our God is a man of war! Wow! Why such a radical stance for this book? I want to establish this precedence:

It Is Wartime!

Throughout the Old Testament, you can find God's name. This provides insight into how God empowers His end-time army to fight and win battles. It helps to become familiar with the names of God. Knowledge of the names of God will help you understand the character and nature of our heavenly Father. It will also help us through life's struggles. The New Testament similarly gives us the name of Jesus Christ. We are given the authority to use it in the spirit realm to fight and win all battles.

Paul told the Church in Ephesus the same thing I am saying to you right now, **"Put on the whole armor of God so that you may be able to stand against the wiles of the enemy!"** (Ephesians 6:11). The Apostle Paul is instructing you so that you will withstand the attack of the enemy. The original

Greek meaning for the word wiles is *methodos*[1] . It refers to the strategies, deceit, and trickery the enemy employs against us.

The satanic world (kingdom) does exist. It is well structured and organized, with strategies or schemes to stop and block you from becoming a vital part of God's army. Undoubtedly, you know the old saying, "What you don't know can't hurt you!". That is not true! It contradicts the word of God. Scripture teaches us, **"My people are destroyed for lack of knowledge"** (Hosea 4:6a). Ignoring truth and rejecting knowledge does not allow us to escape the consequences of sinning against God. Ignorance and rejection of knowledge leads to destruction. God holds us accountable to search for the truth and respond correctly to its demands.

The enemy has an arsenal of strategies for individuals, towns, cities, villages, states, countries, and nations. He wants to put them on *spiritual LOCKDOWN*. The enemy is confronting the Church systematically and strategically using a complex system of deception. Therefore, we cannot face the battle with a humdrum attitude. We cannot ap-

---

1. The Greek definition of the word in Eph. 6:11 wiles or strategies (methodeía) comes from suggest methods, a "way of searching after something, an inquiry; a method), scheming, craftiness" (Bible Hub)

proach Bible study night or Sunday as another
routine service. We cannot simply add cute titles to sermons or have a get-along attitude! It is
WARTIME!

End-Times

Let us look at the second word in my title: End-Time. Please know that God is raising an End-time Army. Some call it the Remnant Church; others call it *The Mighty Apostolic Prophetic Reformation Movement*. Understand that the Holy Spirit empowers us to
be God's End-Time Army. When we talk about
the end times, we are talking about the close of this
age. Time is running out like the fourth quarter of
a sports game. The end is near. In this Laodicean
(lukewarm) church age, I am unsure how many believe that we are in the end times. It does not matter
if they believe it; the signs of the time define where
we are in time. There is no debate about it. I do not
need to prove my point of view on eschatology to
anyone, nor does anyone need to point out their
scriptural viewpoints to me. The clock is ticking,
time is moving on, and it is late. It is the end time! I
will close this portion with the words of the Apostle
Paul, giving more evidence that this is the end time.

Now the Spirit expressly says that in the
latter *times* [END TIMES] some will
depart from the faith, giving heed to de-
ceiving spirits and doctrines of demons
                              1 Timothy 4:1 KJV

The Army Of God

Finally, let us look at the last word, which is Army.
The basic definition for the word army is an organized military force equipped for fighting. Spiritually speaking, it is just that simple. Ready for battle!
Ready to fight! Ready to contend for the faith! Here
is an opportunity for me to interject a prophetic
word. About five years ago, while in prayer, the
Spirit of the Lord spoke to me and said, "I do not
just have a Church. I have an army!". Somebody
ought to say glory to God. There must be a shift
in our mentality (thinking) and functionality (oper-
ation) as the body of Christ. If average believers
would embrace this truth and begin to realize that
the Lord has not called us to passivity, neutrality,
complacency, or mediocrity in this invisible cosmic
battle, their entire concept of the Church would
change! We must take up arms (spiritual weapon-
ry) and fight the good fight of faith! I am talking
about a shift!

Envision what I see right now! I see Churches all across cities and towns functioning as spiritual military facilities. They are headquarters, centers, apostolic centers, and command posts. It means patrons of these ministries must not do Church as usual. They are God's army! By joining the army of the Lord, everything changes! A militant mindset develops. Believers begin to understand that every human being is involved in warfare, whether they realize it or not and whether they actively participate or not!

Spiritual warfare can wear one out because of ignorance, unpreparedness, and not being equipped for battle. The believer must not be ignorant of the enemy's devices to prevent him so he can abuse him, as stated in 2 Corinthians 2:11. We must **"fight the good fight of faith"** (1 Timothy 6:12). Hallelujah! God's End Time Army is rising in these End Times!!!!!!!

The original Greek word for Church (ekklesia) defines the Church as a mobile unit. It is symbolic of the Tabernacle in the wilderness. Therefore, the title of this book exposes something and taps into one of the reasons why today's Church is not mobile. Historically, armies engaged in military conflicts. They are deployed and mobilized to pursue the enemy. Sadly, today's Church is just the opposite. It is mainly stationary and nonconfrontational, with no distinct movement.

Prophecy

The prophet Joel said in Joel 2:11, **"And the Lord shall utter his voice before his army,"** meaning God shall give marching orders to His army like a military leader rallying his troops to battle. The prophet Joel is referring to our present age. He is bringing our attention to God's end-time army. Once you get the revelation of the phrase "before his army," it alludes to a military regiment. Everyone with military experience or knowledge knows that a commanding officer, drill instructor, platoon, or squad leader does not command "Forward March!" or other orders until the soldiers are standing at attention with their weapons properly prepared (battle ready). I want to emphasize that the word Church has been grossly misinterpreted and misunderstood. As kingdom believers, our assignment is not just to go to Church but to be the Church, the *ecclesia*, the called-out ones, deployed as the army of the Lord! The army of God is a force to be reckoned with! Jesus said, **"Upon this rock, I will build my church, and the gates of hell shall not prevail against it"** (Matthew 16:18).

²²For day by day men kept coming to David to help him, until there was a great army, like the army of God.

                          1 Chronicles 12:22 AMP

Believe me, my friend, when we take our rightful place and assignment as the army of the Lord, we will begin to fulfill Joel 2:11. We will become that exceeding great, strong, and mighty army. God's end-time army is not just the title of a book; it is a calling! It is a kingdom assignment! You are called to be more than just another Church on the corner or another preacher in the pulpit. To all of our Church leaders, I want you to see what happened to David. Before he had an army, David was chosen and anointed by God, which aligned him with the Father's will for his life. These factors, along with God's prophetic time clock over his life, inevitably led to a time of prophetic synchronization. Then, supernaturally, God began moving on the hearts of mighty men of valor. These men evolved into the army of God! It is wartime!

A Famous Quote
"I am not afraid of an army of lions led
by a sheep, But I am so scared of an
army of sheep led by a lion."
Alexander The Great

Yes, I'm making a clarion call to those I identify as *The Movement Ministries*: the Evangelists, the Prophets, and the Apostles. These ministries have the assignment to shift the Church from being a sleeping giant to becoming a mighty army of the Lord. Blow the trumpet in Zion and sound the alarm; it is wartime!

Now let us remember what Paul said to the Church at Corinth: "**...the weapons of our warfare are not carnal...**" (2 Corinthians 10:4). The battle we face is neither physical nor a natural fight. It is a spiritual battle! The warfare is for godliness, morality, and godly values. It is an all-out battle against the fullness of the Holy Spirit. In the Old Covenant, God gave his people a ministry called *The Trumpeters' Ministry*, found in Numbers Chapter 10 and other places in scripture. The Trumpeters played an essential role because they summoned the army for battle by blowing the trumpet. In this present time, I consider the Trumpeters the voices of the evangelists and the prophets. When these ministry gifts are most accurate, their messages have a cry, a sound, and an awakening. As we understand the history of Moses and the Joshua generation, God gave them both the Promised Land. Enemies surrounded Moses and Joshua. God gave them the Trumpeter's Ministry to sound an alarm, to awaken the camp, and to declare a call to war. Let's look at Paul said about the Trumpeter's Ministry.

> [8] For if the trumpet gives an uncertain sound, who shall prepare himself for the battle?
>
> 1 Corinthians 14:8 AMP

Wow, that's powerful! In the original Greek, the trumpet is *trompeta*, equivalent to today's war bugle. So, in the above-referenced verse, the King James translation states "an uncertain sound," but it is an indistinct call in the original Greek. There must be a clear-sounding call from the evangelist and or the prophet (the Trumpeter) *to* awaken the Church/the Army of the Lord and prepare them for BATTLE!

If you study the history of most great battles, they were victorious because of a strategy and a time of preparation. Do not forget, **"the battle is not yours, but the Lord's,"** just like He told King Jehoshaphat in 2 Chronicles chapter 20.

15 And he said, Hearken ye, all Judah,
and ye inhabitants of Jerusalem, and
thou king Jehoshaphat, Thus saith
the Lord unto you, Be not afraid nor
dismayed by reason of this great mul-
titude; for the battle is not yours,
but God's. **16** To morrow go ye down
against them: behold, they come up
by the cliff of Ziz; and ye shall find
them at the end of the brook, before
the wilderness of Jeruel. **17** Ye shall
not need to fight in this battle: set
yourselves, stand ye still, and see the
salvation of the Lord with you, O Judah and Jerusalem: fear not, nor be
dismayed; to morrow go out against
them: for the Lord will be with you.

2 Chronicles 20:16-17 KJV

Let us take this step by step because I do not
want to sound like I am saying two different things.
We are the army of the Lord. We do not have to
fight this battle physically with flesh and blood. As
kingdom citizens, we take authority in the realm of
the Spirit and territory in the realm of the Spirit.
We go into the real world, in the realm of the Spirit,
and we fight with the weapons of prayer, praise, and

the spoken word of God through the power of our confession.

By reflecting on 2 Chronicles 20:15- 17, I see something different in verses 15, 16, and 17. In each verse, I want to point out how God speaks to us today. You can see His mighty army through these verses. In verse 15, God says, **"The battle is not yours!"** We have discussed this previously. Stop fighting, and let the word work for you. In verse 16, what God says to the people, **"Tomorrow, go down against them,"** is noteworthy. In the day and time we are living in, we must be willing to confront and challenge the status quo. We can no longer remain passive and inactive in spiritual warfare. We must put on the whole armor of God and take our place and position in this great army and stand (Ephesians 6:10-18)! In verse 16, when we **"stand ye still"**, we will see the salvation of the Lord with us. There is no need to fear or despair. God assures us of His presence and our victory in Him!

The Three P'S Of Wartime: Place, Position, And Purpose

[31]Or what king would go to war against another king without first sitting down to consider whether his ten thousand

soldiers could go up against the twenty
thousand coming against him.

Luke 14:31 CEB

As we conclude this section, remember that the
word tells us no one goes to war or battle until first
sitting down and counting the costs. In the original
Greek, that means sitting down and strategizing. No
astute military General would ever enter a battle
without careful planning, calculation, examination
of available resources and battle strategies. Too
many of us have gone out into kingdom assignments
without sitting down and considering the three Ps
first: Place, Position, and Purpose!

When we think about a place, we immediately
think about a stationary building like a church, office building, or shop space. However, the para-
digm has changed, and we must start to see more
than just a fixed place of worship. God is establish-
ing revival hubs, apostolic centers, networks, and
many mobile ministries that can affect change in
communities. The remnant believer in ministries
must begin to see and understand it is no more
Church as usual. We must indeed start to embrace
the mind of Christ and the wisdom of God. We
must learn how to function in these new types of
ministries. Let us remember what the book of Isaiah
said: **"Behold I do a new thing"** (Isaiah 43:19).

During the American Civil War between the North and the South, did you know that generals on both sides selected a particular ground that appeared to be an excellent place to fight from? I always thought it interesting that, in many cases, they looked for a specific location. Once determined, the General called that Place the *High Ground*. That speaks volumes to you and me today! In the natural, high ground offers the most advantageous position to be on the battlefield. High ground provides an elevated vantage point with a broad field view. The high ground allows the army to see the enemy before the enemy can see them. The military with high ground has better surveillance of the surrounding area and better defense. It is difficult to sneak up or ambush those on high ground.

When I speak about a Place, I am not talking about a physical location. If you look in the book of Genesis and go all the way to the book of Malachi, you will see that there was always a desire to build a place to meet God. The worshipper always calls those unique meeting places ALTARS to God. Now we know the devil, our enemy, will launch an attack from anywhere. In contrast, as believers, we should always work toward attaining and maintaining the spiritual high ground. That is getting into a good place with God. Psalms 24: 3-5 tells us how to obtain the high ground and stay close to God continuously. We never know when another battle will pop up in some area of our lives.

> ¹Whoever dwells in the shelter of the Most High will rest in the shadow of the Almighty. ²I will say of the Lord, "He is my refuge and my fortress, my God, in whom I trust.
>
> Psalm 91:1-2 NIV

I do not know if you have ever looked at Psalms 91 like this, but it becomes a trade-off. I know you are saying "what do you mean?". If you get into a place as suggested in Psalms 91:1 and make that place a dwelling p*lace*, you are guaranteed the promises, protection, and provisions of verses 2-11. The word dwell means to remain somewhere for some time. Dwelling requires interaction, communication, time, and trust. To dwell means to become fully engaged in that Place with God. Verse 2 further explains the benefits and the confidence earned when one takes time to stay in that secret *place*, **"I will say the Lord, He is my refuge, my fortress: my God; in him will I trust"** (Psalm 91:2). So, once we enter a Place, God becomes our protector and the one who fights the battle for us. Therefore, as a Christian believer, I must embrace the revelation of getting into a Place with God. The secret Place *positions* you to win every battle. After all, our heavenly Father raised and seated us in heavenly Places in Christ Jesus (Ephesians 2:6). It is wartime!

> [8]Finally, brothers and sisters, whatever is true, whatever is noble, whatever is right, whatever is pure, whatever is lovely, whatever is admirable—if anything is excellent or praiseworthy—think about such things. [9]Whatever you have learned or received or heard from me or seen in me—put it into practice. And the God of peace will be with you.
>
> Philippians 4:8-9 NIV

The Apostle Paul puts it all in perspective when he says, "Finally, my brethren". The enemy brings us to the battlefield of the mind. Every battle first begins in the mind; either we become victorious in our thinking, or we experience mental defeat.

In verse 8, Paul is telling us to target our thinking. We are to intentionally focus on the things that line up with truth. While amid personal warfare, we must target our thoughts by simply thinking well. That is, having a mindset that aligns with God's word. We target our thinking by meditating on the word of God. Let us remember that human beings are triune. We are made in the image and likeness of God; He is a spirit living in a body and possessing a soul. Amidst battles, the person's soul is challenged, but remember the Lord's words to Jehoshaphat in 2 Chronicles, **"you do not need to fight in this battle!"**. Under the old covenant, God fought battles for His people during wartime. They did physically go to war, but God gave them the victory. The New Testament emphasizes that Jesus Christ, our triumphant victor, has already won the battle.

The Church/The Higher Ground

As Kingdom-minded people and not just another church on the corner, our calling should influence the direction of our lives as naturally as it does spiritually. When we say get to the high ground as kingdom believers, we must mobilize in politics, community activism, and the financial arena called the marketplace. In all these areas, we must possess the higher ground. In this vast world of local, national, and global systems, we must pursue the higher ground, such as Joseph's calling. A Joseph ministry manages and distributes wealth. Indeed, my friend, I believe if we did more than go to Church, we would better understand the greater calling. The more outstanding assignment should be influencing and impacting the political world and the governmental system.

> And the Lord shall make thee the head,
> and not the tail; and thou shalt be above
> only, and thou shalt not be beneath; if
> that thou hearken unto the command-
> ments of the Lord thy God
>   Deuteronomy 28:13 KJV

As we live our daily lives as Christians transitioning from soulish men to spiritual men, I admonish you to guard your minds and understand it is not the enemy's playground but his *war zone*. Cast him out of your mind daily!!!!

> For the weapons of our warfare are not
> carnal, but mighty through God to the
> pulling down of strong holds; Casting
> down imaginations.
>   2 Corinthians 10:4 KJV

Our human nature often challenges us and pulls us back into whatever our worldly financial status dictates. We stay in the realm of sight instead of walking by faith. I have a good revelation for you; you are not the *Moses Generation* that Moses talked and wrote to in the book of Exodus and Numbers. You are the *Joshua* Generation. You are a people with a different *SPIRIT* and well able to take the land. The *Joshua* generation had a better way of thinking and obeying. They could possess the promises of God because they knew their God. But the older generation wanted to go back to Egypt. I love how the book of Daniel chapter 11:32 expresses this fact, **"but the people that do know their God shall be strong, and do exploits."** These are kingdom people who have acquired the high ground!

Globalization is a keyword in today's terminology. Many believe globalization will help markets achieve oneness. Similarly, the kingdom of God is building spiritual influence and unity to become a mighty army! Kingdoms of this world are pursuing a one-world government, a new world order system, a beast system, setting the stage for the antichrist in these end times. It is important to note that the kingdom of God and the global system run parallel. The Holy Spirit is building a mighty kingdom army; conversely, we perceive the establishment of a new world order system. These two armies will collide on a global scale. Paul supports this in scripture by sharing that, **"Every high thing that exalted itself against the knowledge of God, and bringing into captivity every thought to the obedience of Christ"** (2 Corinthians 10:4-5).

A Famous Quote
"Victorious warriors win first, and then go to the war. While defeated warriors go to war first and then seek to win"
                                    Sun Tzu

Every Christian must hear the trumpet declaring: It is wartime! Every believer, not just those in the pulpit, are summoned to the call. The primary goal of this book is to stir up today's Christians and rid them of mediocrity. I want you to ask yourself, "What is my current Spiritual GPS?". Where am I located in my walk with God? Am I pursuing higher spiritual places in the Kingdom of God or have I purchased an unlimited stay at the Laodicean Christian Inn where I can have it my way? Today, many believe in a self centered Christianity. No, my friends, hear and understand the heart of the Apostle Paul in Ephesians 1:21. Christ has been seated or positioned *FAR ABOVE* our adversary, the devil!

> [20]Which he wrought in Christ, when he raised him from the dead, and set him at his own right hand in the heavenly places, [21]far above all principality, and power, and might, and dominion, and every name that is named, not only in this world, but also in that which is to come: [22]And hath put all things under

his feet, and gave him to be the head
over all things to the Church, [23]Which
is his body, the fulness of him that filleth
all in all.

Ephesians 1:20-23 KJV

Glory to God! Let us get two words into our spirits: far above. Yes, far above. To do this justice, we
must go back to the 17th verse of the same chapter
to fully understand what the great Apostle Paul is
praying by the Spirit of the Lord. Paul's prayer reveals something powerful! He prays that God will
give us **"the spirit of wisdom and revelation in
the knowledge of him,"** i.e., Christ. The depth of
his intimacy with Christ and spiritual experiences
truly astounds us. The abundance of revelation and
the magnitude of his spiritual understanding stag-
gers our imagination. There were things he had
experienced that were inexpressible and forbid-
den to tell (2 Corinthians 12: 1-4). My friend, we
must receive revelation that we are seated far above
principalities and powers because we are seated
"together in heavenly places in Christ Jesus!"
(Ephesians 2:6). This incredible revelation changes
how we think! Remember, in the beginning, we
talked about the Church mindset versus an army
mindset. I told you that God spoke to me and said,
"I do not have a Church; I have an army!". Remem-

ber, the weapons of our warfare are not carnal but mighty to pull down all strongholds through God. If you go back and read Ephesians 1:21, the Apostle Paul breaks this down. He identifies that we are seated far above all: principality, power, dominion, might, and every name named in this present world and the world to come. My God! He did not leave anything out! Are you able to comprehend this? We are far above anything that will confront us in this world and the future. My God! My God! To strengthen our case by referencing "far above", Paul reveals this truth in chapter four of the same book.

> [10]He that descended is the same also that ascended up *far above* all heavens, that he might fill all things.
>
>   Ephesians 4:10 KJV

It is wartime! As a soldier in the army of the Lord, I must see and understand who my enemy is. I must get to higher ground. I must place myself in a proper position. People often get to higher ground and do as Peter did on the mount of transfiguration.

> [1]And after six days Jesus taketh Peter, James, and John his brother, and bringeth them up into a high moun-

tain apart, [2]and was transfigured before them: and his face did shine as
the sun, and his raiment was white as
the light. [3]And, behold, there appeared
unto them Moses and Elias talking with
him. [4]Then answered Peter, and said
unto Jesus, Lord, it is good for us to be
here: if thou wilt, let us make here three
tabernacles; one for thee, and one for
Moses, and one for Elias.

Matthew 17:1-4 KJV

You can read Matthew chapter 17:1-4 and see
what Peter did wrong. He did what we all do when
we get into a place with God, and God is ready to
bless us. We talk too much instead of being still and
waiting on the Lord. Instead of talking, we should
just enjoy the experience encountering His presence.

We are often guilty, like Peter, who famously said,
"It is good for us to be here". Many people do that
every Sunday morning when they go to Church.
However, the Church is supposed to be an equipping station. It is a place of impartation and activation. This book is written for all of us to become
God's end-time army. We are mighty warriors fit for
battle. Our mindsets have to shift from saying, "It
was good for us to be here; our Pastor brought forth
a powerful word today".

Remember, armies move out; they mobilize, strategize, and deploy. They do not show up at the same location week after week and say, "We had a good time this morning, and I enjoyed the choir". Do not get me wrong, I have been a pastor and worked with many pastors. I know what David said in the book of Psalms, **"I was glad when they said unto me let us go into the House of the Lord" (Psalm 122:1).** My point is that, going to the House of the Lord is not only for a good time. Our going is to be equipped and trained!

Once I reach higher ground in the Spirit, I must embrace these three principles for wartime success: 1. Place, 2. Position, and 3. Purpose. Those who have military backgrounds know that this is a military procedure. There are several good examples throughout military history as you do your research on historical battles. Good leaders will establish the three P's: Place, Position, and Purpose.

3

LET'S GET TO HIGHER GROUND

LET'S GET TO HIGHER GROUND

Isaiah 2:2
And it shall come to pass in the last days, that
the mountain of the Lord's house shall be
established in the top of the mountains,
and shall be exalted above
the hills; and all nations
shall flow unto it.

Is Today's Church Losing?

At this point, we may ask, "Is today's Church losing?". The answer is in the realm of the soul: the mind, will, and emotions. However, many are mentally seated in the wrong position. This is due to ignorance and the lack of application of God's word. At the same time, spiritually, the finished work of Christ has given us a position of authority and an inheritance. Jesus' resurrection was with power and authority; He visited Hell and took the keys of the kingdom from the enemy, the devil.

The book of **Hosea 4:6 states, "My people are destroyed for lack of knowledge".** Yet, some people say, "What I do not know will not hurt me". This is untrue. What you do not know still has the potential to hurt you. The leading cause for our failure is the words from our mouths. What comes out of our mouths generates in our hearts, goes through our brain, and then is released into our atmosphere. James chapter 3 will illustrate why today's Church is experiencing defeat.

> [5]Even so, the tongue is a little member and boasteth great things. Behold, how great a matter a little fire kindleth! [6]And the tongue is a fire, a world of iniquity: so is the tongue among our members,

that it defileth the whole body, and set-
teth on fire the course of nature; and it
is set on fire of Hell.

James 3:5-6 KJV

Let us reflect on where we are at this point. Chapter 3 is about Getting to Higher Ground. I am re-
dundant, but I must emphasize that Jesus Christ
purchased high ground with his sacrificial death
and resurrection power. His sacrifice makes us vic-
tors. Yet, believers struggle in their relationships,
finances, and spiritual matters. James 3:6 points to
that trouble area, saying that the tongue is a "fire".
When you think about a fire, you think about something that can spark something and spread rapidly.
This is the case with the words we release from our
mouths. Are they starting things on the earth for
you or against you? Remember, words govern the
kingdom of God. We must never forget that! Jesus
said that the words He speaks are "spirit and life"
(John 6:63). Remember, words can bring death or
life (Proverbs 18:21).

A Famous Quote
"Words are the coins that make up the
currency of a sentence, and there are
always too many small coins."

Jules Renard

For those familiar with the Hebrew calendar, in
2020, we entered the Jewish year 5780 (2020). The
number 80 is equivalent to the Hebrew letter "PEY".
This Hebraic letter "PEY" resembles a mouth. It
means to express and vocalize. Therefore, 5780
was declared "the Year of the Mouth". Many prominent apostolic and prophetic voices concurred with
that prophetic word. So, as God's people, I want
to encourage you. The prophetic word received in
2020, "the Year of the Mouth," is still relevant in this
season. We are to make declarations and decrees
to speak the word of faith and to take God at His
promises. We must meditate on God's words and
revert those faith declarations to Him. You will begin to see Jeremiah 1:12 manifest in your life. God
will start to hasten His word to perform it on your
behalf if you speak only His word in this season.

The Church has lost ground because many
Churchgoers have religiously perceived its purpose. People are busy going to Church instead of
getting the revelation of God's purpose for His
Church. Believers are the Church. Believers must

execute their assignment to function as ambassadors of God's kingdom under the leadership of the Holy Spirit. If today's Church looks into a mirror, would there be a reflection of the early Church in the Book of Acts? Unfortunately, there would be no comparison! If we open our spiritual eyes, we will see a vast difference between the early Church and today's Church. It is elementary! The early Church was the Church on display with God's power and glory. The Church moved from display to demonstrations! The Church of the end time will be the same. The glory of the latter house shall exceed the former. Ephesians chapter 5 tells us that God is looking for a glorious Church, a holy Church, without a spot, wrinkle, and without blemish. Glory to God! It is also called the Remnant Church. Glory to God! I sense the presence of the Lord!

> [2]And a certain man lame from his mother's womb was carried, whom they laid daily at the gate of the temple which is called Beautiful, to ask alms of them that entered into the temple; [3]who seeing Peter and John about to go into the temple asked an alms. [4]And Peter, fastening his eyes upon him with John, said, Look on us. [5]And he gave heed unto them, expecting to receive something of them. [6]Then Peter said,

> Silver and gold have I none; but such as I have to give I thee: In the name of Jesus Christ of Nazareth, rise up and walk.
>
> Acts 3:2-6 KJV

Wow! There is so much to be said here. The Church must see itself as the gatekeeper to the world. Peter comes in contact with a man at the temple. The man represents a type of the world. He is going through an extended personal dilemma. He was lame from birth, always needing somebody to help him. However, if the one who proposes to be a helper needs help them-self, he cannot give help to another. Therefore, the Church must be victorious because it must be the help of a dying world. The man at the temple needed a healing miracle. Peter said to him, "Look on us!". Wow! That will preach!!!!

The Church today is rising to become a "look on us" Remnant Generation. The Holy Spirit compels and propels us to the forefront of the kingdom of God in ministry today. The early apostles were the Remnants of their day. The Church is today's Remnant. The first apostles had three years of preparation for their moment. Prophetically, today's Remnant generation must utilize the tools of preparation: prayer, fasting, and consuming the word of

God. It should be all about getting into a place with God!

Again, I address this question, "Why is today's Church losing?". In Acts Chapter 3, Apostles Peter and John were in a great spiritual place. They were on higher ground spiritually. They did not just walk into the temple as mere men but as two powerful men of God. Case in point, all Peter had to say to the lame man was, "Look on us!". He boldly spoke to the lame man because he was in a spiritually high place of authority.

As a covenant believer, I remind you that this same power is available for all believers to experience and walk in today. Mark chapter 16 says that signs follow those who believe in Jesus Christ. I am sure you heard the phrase, "It is all in your mind" or "The mind is the devil's playground". From a kingdom perspective, we have already won every battle through Christ! Nevertheless, we are defeating ourselves by the way we think and talk. Stop now and self-check your mind, will, and emotions. There may be an issue in one of these three areas in your life. You may be suffering silently and unaware of it. I have provided a questionnaire below so that you can test your mind, will, and emotions.

Test Yourself

1. Do you wrestle mentally with negative/evil thoughts? [Yes] [No] (The Mind)

2. Do you feel frustrated about going around the same circles in life? [Yes] [No] (The Emotions)

3. Do you wrestle with always having to be in control of things? [Yes] [No] (The Will)

This test will help you evaluate where you are in your mind, will, and emotions. While we may be spiritually gifted and anointed by God, at the same time, we may be losing in the area of our souls. We see it repeatedly on Sundays; people come to Church with hidden issues in their hearts but never overcome them. In this next section, I want to talk about the carnal Christian. Sadly, that is a large percentage of today's Church. As a result, we are losing! Hang out with me and keep reading. I know this hurts, but it will help sooner than later. Just think about a natural army. When you join the military, your starting point is boot camp. The army's assignment is to change your mindset about who you are. It provides the necessary tools for your development and performance as a soldier. The military tells you that you are a loser, a nobody, but we will make you somebody! It is a place of discipline and transformation with many military rules, regulations, laws, and orders you must follow.

Basic training is initially challenging; however, if you persevere, there is a graduation date. You will put on your decorated uniform, look dapper with your polished weapon, and parade before hundreds applauding you on graduation day. What a sense of great pride and accomplishment as you march with your platoon. Wow! It is such an incredible feeling and ostentatious moment! I am sure you have seen it often; Uncle Sam's army soldiers are now trained, equipped, and ready for battle!

Carnal Christianity: The Enemies Weapon

In North America, carnal Christianity has invaded the ranks of the Church as we know it today. For example, if a brother or sister in Christ is passionate about prayer and fasting as a lifestyle and is inspired to live a consecrated life, the majority of Christians would look at them and say, "It doesn't take all of that. God's grace fills in all the blanks". Carnal Christianity needs to be exposed today. The early Church was on fire for God and governed by men of God who lived a consecrated life. Even the great Apostle Paul, who brought forth the grace message, says, "**I am crucified with Christ: nevertheless I live**" (Galatians 2:20). Apostle Paul went on to exhort us, "**I beseech you therefore, brethren, by the mercies of God, that ye present your bodies a living sacrifice**" (Romans 12:1). Apostle Paul urged us to present ourselves as consecrated vessels that will be holy and pleasing to God. I am just paraphrasing it; I encourage you to read Romans chapter 12:1-4. We will spiritually lose if we do not seek the Lord in consecration. As humans, our innate nature will automatically kick in, dominate, and control our lives. Today's Church is stuck in a Laodicean mindset because of a prevailing unbalanced grace message. To reawaken this great sleeping giant, the Church must hear from her authentic voices: the prophets. During this season, a new breed of voices is rising. The voices are types of Jeremiah and John the Baptist. They will bring a renewed message to the Church. They will boldly speak of holiness, righteousness, and godliness. Those who belong to the Church are more than conquerors because of Christ's finished work. We are not a losing Church! We have already won!

> [1]However, brothers and sisters, I could not talk to you as to spiritual people, but [only] as to worldly people [dominated by human nature], *mere* infants [in the new life] in Christ! [2]I fed you

with milk, not solid food; for you
were not yet able *to receive it.* Even
now, you are still not ready. [3]You
are still worldly [controlled by ordinary impulses, the sinful capaci-
ty]. For as long as there is jeal-
ousy, strife, *and* discord among you,
are you not unspiritual, and are you
not walking like ordinary men [un-
changed by faith]?

                    1 Corinthians 3:1-3 AMP

Please note that in the Amplified Version of this
chapter, verse 3 refers to carnality as being worldly,
while the King James Version says, "For ye are yet
carnal". Either way, it is an issue that must be identified and addressed. If we want to move forward
as the army of the Lord, we have to tackle carnal Christianity. The name of this book expresses
it clearly: The Army of the Lord! No army gives
loaded weapons to babies. According to the word
of God, carnal Christians are called babes in Christ.
Review 1 Corinthians 3:1. The original Greek definition of carnal Christians was infants or babies. In
verse 2, Paul points out that because we are infants
or spiritual babies, we cannot receive solid food
from the word of God. When we do not get the
proper nutrition, we cannot grow. I love how the

Apostle Paul addresses Christians and the
Church in 1 Corinthians 3:16. It is a scriptural exit
strategy.

> [16]Know ye not that ye are the temple
> of God, and that the Spirit of God
> dwelleth in you?
>
> 1 Corinthians 3:16 KJV

Telling carnally minded Christians that the Spirit of God dwells within them provides hope for
them. However, we must take it a step further. We
can help carnal Christians overcome and defeat
carnality by showing how they grieve the Holy
Spir-it. We must let them know that they must repent. Paul tells us to **"grieve not the Holy Spirit
which is the earnestness of our inheritance"**
(Ephesians 4:30). Repentance is the down pay-
ment or the bridge that takes us from flesh to a
victorious life in the spirit. Please note Ephesians
4:30 and meditate on what Paul says: **"Grieve not
the Holy Spirit"**. You may see why this is a master
key; this is an exit strategy. When we grieve Him,
we live as carnal believers. Even though He dwells
within us, we become a slave to our human nature.

As we proceed, I want to discuss the three R's:
Repentance, Revive, and Recover. These will all
occur when you understand the power that dwells

within you through the Holy Spirit. It all starts with repentance.

Repentance closes the door to living in the flesh and being controlled by one's carnal nature. As a result, you can live and walk in the Spirit of God. Once you have crossed the bridge of repen-tance, you can experience joy, revival, and spiritual awakenings.

Revival makes us think about big camp meetings, mega conferences, and a guest speaker. However, revival can also be a very personal experience. When revived, Christians live in a revival atmosphere: on fire for God.

The third 'R' means to Recover; a synonymous term is restoration or to restore. Our Father God gives us a promise in the book of Joel 2:25: "I will restore." This is a prophetic promise to embrace today in your life. Once you do so, you are ready for the next phase: Marching Up The Hill

Marching Up The Hill

The End-time Army of the Lord must have the Holy Spirit. They must have the encounter of Acts chapter 2. They must be ready to go and empowered to move beyond the pews of the Church. In Matthew 28:19, Jesus says, "**Go ye**". How did we miss that? We must go, go again, and keep going!

Whatever village or city you live in is your region or territory; that is your domain. So go and take dominion! Do the work of an evangelist and make full proof of your ministry! Put your prophecies on the shelf, your dreams in your back pocket, and your visions in a safe place. These are all of the Lord! They will come to pass if you obey the call to GO.

God told me that He does not merely have a church but an Army. Start meditating on the fact that you are not a member of the Church, but you are apart of an Army. That army is called the body of Christ. The first time I heard that comment by the Spirit of the Lord, I was shocked too! However, it makes sense! That revelation made me more focused.

One of the first things that soldiers learn is how to stand at attention and march. Marching helps soldiers keep pace and stay in alignment with the person who is called the team leader. I am sure you have seen a group of soldiers marching in unison together. In front, someone carries the team leader's flag. In the kingdom, team leaders are called Pastors, Teachers, Evangelists, Prophets, and Apostles.

When you think of great military battles, you envision a small group marching together in unison up a hill. It is a demonstration of the power of agreement. If you disagree, you cannot march up the mountain. Many of our ministries need to be

authentically united. We must hear the cry of Nehemiah, which I will discuss in the next paragraph.

> [17]Then said I unto them, Ye see the dis-
> tress that we are in, how Jerusalem lieth
> waste and the gates thereof are burned
> with fire: come, and let us build up the
> wall of Jerusalem, that we bare no more
> a reproach. [18]Then I told them of the
> hand of my God which was good upon
> me; as also the king's words that he had
> spoken unto me. And they said, let us
> rise and build. So, they strengthened
> their hands for this good work.
>
> Nehemiah 2:17-18 KJV

One man created an army, marched back into his
city, and rebuilt it. God calls believers to march into
their cities, towns, and villages to possess the land
in Jesus' name. There are many things I could point
out about Nehemiah, but the main thing I want you
to see is that Nehemiah was a great leader. He is
a tremendous apostolic type for today's apostolic
and prophetic leadership. Not only did he have
favor with God and the people, but he had it with
his government and the nation's king. Now that's
Kingdom Apostolic!

Another thing I want to point out about Nehemiah is that he had a burden regarding the condition

of his hometown. Real soldiers in an army have a passion for a cause. Love for a cause should start in Jerusalem: your home base location. In Luke chapter 24, Jesus told his disciples to go to Jerusalem first. He sent them back to their home base to take territory, march up the hill, and possess the land. I want to emphasize that we must start marching up the mountain and take the land where God has placed us first. Too many people want to win the world and go to the nations but leave their cities, towns, or villages in ruin. We can learn a lot from Nehemiah's awareness and response. One of the most important things we need to consider is whether it favors him to return to his home. Under normal circumstances, he did not need to be concerned since he no longer lived there. However, the king recognized Nehemiah's interest and the dire circumstances of his people in their homeland, so he granted him the favor to go and make a difference.

I want to discuss further Nehemiah chapter 2 and verse 17. We first see Nehemiah asking his people if they see the need and the distress. Look at something similar in Luke chapter 19: Jesus beheld his city Jerusalem by the mountain. The Bible says He wept over it because they did not know that the time of the Lord's visitation was at hand! Hear my heart as a prophet of the Lord and not just the author of this book. Our cities are in ruins in

America, and the Church is fast asleep. As a result, the Church will miss the visitation day and the Holy Spirit's beckoning call. That clarion call is for the remnant army of the Lord to take up arms and fight to take kingdom dominion.

Nehemiah's second emphasis was on the destruction of the city's gates. We could write many books about the gates of regions and how the enemy has infiltrated them through destructive forces like moral decay, gender identity, racial issues, and the spirit of the antichrist.

As the mighty army of the Lord, we must march forward into enemy territory and confront the gates of regions. We must have an apostolic and a prophetic understanding of territories and how to move in and out of the spirit world as elite high priest intercessors of the Lord! Many have taken on titles and need help understanding the authority and the responsibility in the spirit realm of their titles. They endeavor to confront the spirits of the enemy's camp but do not have heaven's backing to move into those spheres. My friends, even the great apostle Paul wrote much of the new covenant. He understood he had a metron or a sphere of influence for his kingdom assignment.

[18]And I say also unto thee, that thou art
Peter, and upon this rock, I will build
my Church; and the *gates* of Hell shall
not prevail against it.

Matthew 16:18 KJV

Right now, the larger question for the Church is,
"Why are the gates of Hell prevailing?". Let us look
at our subtitle: Marching Up The Hill. All military
people know that they must assemble before there
is a march. The army cannot just stand at attention.
The squad leader gives a command to prepare for
the march, and then he provides a cadence in the
squad to commence the march following the squad
leader. Now, let us shift that to the local Church.
Firstly, we need to ensure who is in charge and
who has the authority. If the individual is not the
leader, the army will never respond to the call to
assemble. Oh my God, I just said something! If you
do not believe me, read the verse below in the book
of Corinthians chapter 14. Paul told the Church
at Corinth about the trumpet: the calling of the
assembly/army of the Lord.

⁸For if the trumpet gives an uncertain
sound, who shall prepare himself for
the battle?

1 Corinthians 14:8 KJV

As the president of a Christian network, I have
traveled to many cities. It has always been my
mission to bring the body of Christ together.
However, the narrative from city to city is the
same 80 to 90% of the time. When there is no
unity within the leadership, there is no marching
army for a cause. As a result, cities look nice to
own from the outside, but as in Nehemiah's time,
the town became a place of ruin. It Is Time To
March Up The Hill.

Marching Forward From Your Kingdom Place

³Blessed be the God and Father of our
Lord Jesus Christ, who hath blessed
us with all spiritual blessings in heavenly places.

Ephesians 1:3 KJV

We understand that our Father has blessed and empowered us to sit in heavenly places. It means believers should elevate their minds to walk and live in heavenly places. This is a finished work. The promises of God are all a completed work. The Lord has finished this work! Believers must enter that place and be seated in our Father's presence. I like how the amplified Bible powerfully expresses it. King James states *Heavenly Places*, while the Amplified Bible says *Heavenly Realms*.

Please note that you have a seat in a high place in the heavenly realm. At the beginning of this chapter, we had to address why we are losing as a Church. As we conclude this chapter, remember that you are a kingdom citizen. Recognize your position and heavenly authority, and march forward. I must stress this point because too many God-fearing Christians are living like the people of the world. They do not recognize their spiritual inheritance.

The finished work of Jesus Christ has offered believers many, many benefits. Wow! It is like being a billionaire, and yet you will not even stop by the bank to access all that belongs to you. I encourage my readers to reposition themselves spiritually. Allow your will to be the will of God. Accept the finished work of the cross. If the Word of God says, "I am seated in heavenly places and have been given an inheritance" simply believe and receive it. As each one in the Army of the Lord sits in that seat of authority, the battle becomes the Lord's.

Let me provide another example. In an orchestra, you compete with others to play the same instrument. There is an intense competition to be seated as a musician in that orchestra; it is an esteemed position. Remember this point when you see the next concert or exceptional TV performance. You are listening to the best of the best! Musicians must earn their seats through countless hours of practice to be considered for such an honorable seat. Let us all remember that Christ did the work for us. The best I can do is embrace the finished work of the cross. By faith in Christ Jesus, I must take my rightful place of authority.

In the past, the military fought all wars on the ground. It was later that the army added a series of fighter jets. The American Civil War is a perfect example; everything was a ground attack. Later, the Air Force was seen in action in World War One and World War Two. As a result, the scene became more powerful. Let us get an excellent Spiritual understanding to see how Jesus' earthly ministry laid the groundwork for us. Thank you, Holy Ghost!

A Famous Quote

Everything negative- pressure, challenges are all an opportunity for me to rise.

Kobe Bryant

4

UNDERSTANDING SPIRITUAL RANKINGS & AUTHORITIES

UNDERSTANDING SPIRITUAL
RANKING & AUTHORITIES

Psalms6
For promotion cometh neither from
the east, nor from the west,
nor from the south.

In the Kingdom of God and the kingdoms of this world, believers must know who the authority figures are. When authorities are not recognized, judgments follow. At the beginning of this chapter, we will discuss spiritual rankings and authorities. First, let us discuss the authorities. The word understanding means grasping the significance of a thing. As we look at our society today, we can see an endless list of authorities being misunderstood and abused. Authorities in this natural world are facing significant challenges. In the Army of the Lord, this is an area where the devil seeks to set up a stronghold. We can only move forward if we establish a leader and core leadership.

I guarantee you that most people in the body of Christ do not even believe there is a spiritual ranking level of authority. Yes. It is okay to use the terms of endearment, brother and sister in the Lord, but let us not get it twisted. There is an order and a protocol in the Kingdom of God. I want my readers of this book, God's Army, to begin to grasp the revelation of spiritual ranking in the territories where God has placed them. For example, everyone lives in a city, a town, or a village. The people who sit in the gates, meaning the city's elders, have been spiritually overseeing (manning) those gates by way of authority granted by heaven.

1 After this I looked, and, behold, a door was opened in heaven: and the first voice which I heard was as it were of a trumpet talking with me; which said, Come up hither, and I will shew thee things which must be hereafter. **2** And immediately I was in the spirit: and, behold, a throne was set in heaven, and one sat on the throne. **3** And he that sat was to look upon like a jasper and a sardine stone: and there was a rainbow round about the throne, in sight like unto an emerald. **4** And round about the throne were four and twenty seats: and upon the seats I saw four and twenty elders sitting, clothed in white raiment; and they had on their heads crowns of gold.

Revelation 4:1-4 KJV

The ultimate authority is God our Father. He rules from His throne. Today, many forget that God reigns in full authority and power. It is not like what the tag people used to put on their cars that say, "God is my co-pilot". Whoever made that tag should repent! God is the author and the finisher of all of our faiths! If we understand authority and spiritual rankings, we must first recognize who is in charge. Our Father's throne is in heaven, as we see in Revelation chapter 4. If you do a total word study on the word thrones, you will be amazed how much this word is mentioned in the word of God.

It is amazing how the world taps into heavenly things and uses them the wrong way. You have probably heard of the game called the Game of Thrones. They have the right concept and recognize authorities, but it is twisted up. Yes. Satan, the devil, got it twisted and wanted to set up his throne. Bible history shows us he was swiftly dealt with. Well, you and I both know we have people in the body of Christ and leadership constantly trying to set up their thrones of authority. There are countless examples in the word of God when a person usurped authority. Because of their disobedience, judgment followed. Let me clarify the importance of walking obedient to authority as a child of God. If you are a minister walking in disobedience, you will miss the opportunity for a promotion in spiritual rankings. Let us break down the scriptures I have below. I will also give you the most outstanding examples of spiritual ranking, authority, and what not to do in regards to them.

12 How art thou fallen from heaven, O Lucifer, son of the morning! how art thou cut down to the ground, which didst weaken the nations! 13 For thou hast said in thine heart, I will ascend

into heaven, I will exalt my throne above the stars of God: I will sit also upon the mount of the congregation, in the sides of the north: **14** I will ascend above the heights of the clouds; I will be like the most High.

Isaiah 14:12-14 KJV

First and foremost, Lucifer was the highest spiritually ranking person in the history of heaven. That was good enough. Go back, research, and study the word of God. You will see that he was the highest-ranking angel and was not satisfied with the ranking delegated to him. He did something that all of us have done before: "He said in his heart". Anytime you are in authority, whether in the natural, on a job, in the church, or whatever you do, always check yourself and examine your heart. Examining your heart means to check your mind and your motives. The apostle Paul said it like this, "examine yourselves" (2 Corinthians 13). Keep yourself on the heart examination table when addressing spiritual rankings and authority. Examine yourself, check yourself, and guard your heart!

The second thing he says in verse 13 is crazy, but when you get in the spirit of pride, you start thinking crazy thoughts! He was already spiritually arranged. It is as hard as he could be, and he dared to say, "I will exalt my throne above the stars of God" which means that he planned to put his authority above the authority of his creator. I know that does not make any sense; pride causes your heart to think crazy thoughts.

Remember, we are talking about understanding authority. You must recognize authority to climb the spiritual ladder of higher ranking.

We may get to this before we close out this book, but I was given spiritual ranking and authority in this life. We are going into my eternal life, and I will live out my eternal life in that place of spiritual rank and authority. In other words, you get rewarded for your obedience in the earthly realm.

Lucifer makes an outlandish statement. In verse 13, he said I will exalt my throne above God's throne, which is impossible to do, but pride is a killer. Then, in verse 14, he says I will be like the most high. All persons in the Kingdom already have their DNA and purpose. They should be on assignment. You do not have to be like anyone else. Verse 14 causes many persons in the body of Christ to never come into their place of authority because they are trying to take on another person's DNA in the Kingdom. Similar to our fingerprints, they will never match. I met many people over the years who have wasted valuable time saying what Lucifer said in their hearts: "I will be like so and so".

A Famous Quote
Unthinking respect for authority is the
greatest enemy of truth
Albert Einstein

So here we have the highest-ranking angel that our heavenly Father created, in absolute splendor and amazement. He had a complete orchestra built into him, and he was magnificent. However, your heart's pride never lets you rest and be satisfied with how our Father created you. When a person gets a position of authority, that person must not let the position get into their head. The wisest thing to say is they freeze over several times over the years. Instead, one should become a servant leader. It means that if I am the leader, I am in a position of authority, but my heart is engaged to serve in a leadership capacity. We have got to embrace our leadership role of authority in this manner because this is the way spiritual rankings work. When the seasons of promotion come, as said in Psalm 75, our promotion will come from the Lord. We would not get passed by because our heart would be in the right place. The scripture says it best in Matthew 8 when the centurion came to Jesus Christ. He was a man of authority, but his position of authority did not mess up his heart.

The Lord's Anointed In Authority

⁴ And the men of David said unto him,
Behold the day of which the Lord said
unto thee, Behold, I will deliver thine
enemy into thine hand, that thou
mayest do to him as it shall seem good
unto thee. Then David arose, and cut
off the skirt of Saul's robe privily. ⁵ And
it came to pass afterward, that David's
heart smote him, because he had cut
off Saul's skirt. ⁶ And he said unto his
men, The Lord forbid that I should do
this thing unto my master, the Lord's
anointed, to stretch forth mine hand
against him, seeing he is the anointed of
the Lord. ⁷ So David stayed his servants
with these words, and suffered them
not to rise against Saul. But Saul rose up
out of the cave, and went on his way.

1 Samuel 24:4-7 KJV

Now, Saul and David's dilemma paints a perfect
picture of spiritual ranking in authority displayed
at its best. Should I say what to do and what not to
do? Let us go to the 24th chapter of 1 Samuel. David
had the opportunity to take Saul's life. As history

tells it, Saul was the king; he was the authority and he had the spiritual ranking. David was a shepherd boy with no authority and no ranking. What amazes me is that earlier in this story, we are told that God looks at the heart, not at one's title. I am discussing spiritual ranking in this series, so I do not want us to get caught up on titles and positions.

I read from Bishop Bill Hamon's book that "the last move of God will be the saints' move of God". The saints are people in the body of Christ with no apparent rank or authority. In these end times, God will use them like he used David: an unassuming saint who took on that day's spiritual forces. It is sad to say that there are a lot of Sauls out there today. They have on the garment, the title, and man-given authority. I did not say God-given; I said man-given! Nevertheless, within a day, the scripture tells us that the House of David became stronger and stronger, and the House of Saul became weaker and weaker. Right before our eyes, we see part of the church, called the remnant army of the Lord, take on God-given authority. I want to dwell on Saul and David's dilemma for a minute. I have had to walk through some Saul days as David. As a David company of believers and future leaders, we must understand that our future rule of authority in the Kingdom in spiritual ranking has everything to do with how we handle the person who has the spiritual ranking and authority. Some people question why God put David under Saul's authority while knowing his heart was not right. Hold on to your seats. It might hurt! God puts the Davids under the Sauls to get Sauls' heart out of the David. SELAH!

What you do with your authority today will affect your spiritual ranking tomorrow or in the future. It would have affected David's future if he had not handled that situation the way he did. You should stop right here and repent. People may be in your life, but you did not handle the problem correctly. I am talking Kingdom now. Authority is authority and protocol is protocol in the Kingdom of God. According to Romans 13, the word of God says the powers that be, meaning the authority, have been put there by God. How can I break it down to you? I can not explain everything, but I can tell you that God is in charge. It is not like the tag we used to put on our cars that said, "God is our co-pilot". No, my friends, He is not the co-pilot! He made the raw materials that make up the plane. He made the clouds the plane flies through in the air and the planet that the plane flies on. That qualifies Him to be more than the co-pilot. Please take that tag off the front of your car!

The last thing I want to point out in this section comes from verse 5, which says "David's heart smote him", which means it convicted him that he had come against the Lord's anointed. Not only did that happen to David, but a powerful thing also happened. His mighty men of war wanted to go ahead and take King Saul out themselves, and David stopped them. My fellow leaders can appreciate this chapter. You must be a leader to appreciate this chapter and see how David respects authority. It moves authority!

Spiritual Ranking & Authority Takes Us To Higher Ground

> **3** Therefore came all the elders of Israel to the king to Hebron; and David made a covenant with them in Hebron before the Lord; and they anointed David king over Israel, according to the word of the Lord by Samuel. **4** And David and all Israel went to Jerusalem, which is Jebus; where the Jebusites were, the inhabitants of the land. **5** And the inhabitants of Jebus said to David, Thou shalt not come hither. Nevertheless David took the castle of Zion, which is the city of David.
>
> 1 Chronicles 11:3-5 KJV

This brief story of King David seated as king over all of Israel is tremendous on several prophetic fronts!

According to 1 Chronicles chapter 11, the Elders and others in authority recognized and remembered the prophecy from the prophet Samuel. Samuel was recognized and highly esteemed among the people of that day. They rehearsed the prophecy to David, saying Jehovah has already spoken it through the prophet that you will be our king. It is incredible how people today give themselves titles and positions; this is so ungodly and unscriptural. The Kingdom of God has an absolute protocol and procedure. David knew the prophecy came from God and waited for the manifestation. That is why David succeeded in his reign as king and why the people respected his rank and authority. David responded to challenges toward his reign correctly.

I also want to point out in 1 Chronicles 11:5 how David, the newly seated king, took his authority and possessed the land. We are all kings and priests seated in heavenly places. We are given spiritual authority and rights to move about in the spirit realm. I have the authority to operate my Air Force unit. I want to dwell on this fact for a few minutes. As we know, David would not settle for less than Zion. History tells us Zion was a city on a mountainside, a great location to have your military headquarters because you could always see the enemy coming. So this hits home when we say the City of David or Zion. It is the perfect higher-ground typology. Let me ask you a question, "Have you settled for a low place in your Christian walk?". If so, take a moment to stop, pray, and repent.

My prayer for you: Father, in Jesus' name, thank you that your word says, "If any man is in Christ, he is a new creature; old things are passed away". I pray for my readers. Father, set them on high ground during this time of repentance. Let them experience a prophetic resetting. Reset their minds and their hearts. Thank You that we are kings and priests unto You through the precious blood of the lamb. In Jesus' name, Amen.

Now, as we move onto higher ground, remember David had incredible tenacity; we must have the same. He would not take no for an answer from his enemy. David took the city of Zion. Get that into your spirit. You are already on higher ground. Jesus has already taken the high ground for us. We need to operate as kings and priests by embracing the position of royalty in spirit at all times.

Anytime you get involved in an excellent job at a good company, they introduce you to their first chain of command. In the Old Testament, you had the system of the prophet, the priest, and the king. Whether they got along or not, they all understood the ranking and protocol in the established order system. In 1 Corinthians 12:28, we put a significant premium on the office of the apostle being first and understanding spiritual ranking. We must get a revelation of the verse before, verse 27, "**Now are you**

the body of Christ!". Paul wrote by the Holy Ghost and said it is already established. Once you recognize who you are in the body of Christ, you have your authority and your ranking. You become a new creation in Christ Jesus. I love what one man of God said, "you already got it!". New spiritual rankings are a fascinating topic with a lot of depth to it because, under the old covenant, the same levels of authority exist. They had no access to the Spiritual realm. On the contrary, under the new covenant, the word of God tells us we are under a covenant with better promises. I like to say, "God opens up the entire spiritual realm to the believer in the new covenant".

Our enemy, the devil, tries to devalue our spiritual authority. He knows that Jesus took away from him the keys of death, Hell, and the grave. He knows that we are joint heirs with Christ Jesus. Do not let the enemy convince you otherwise. All of the promises of God are yes and amen. Indeed, let me remind you that we are under a better covenant than King David because it is through the name of Jesus Christ and His precious blood. Our manifestation starts in the spirit world and is manifested in the natural world. You see, my friend, the devil already knows that we are more than conquerors because of the cross and the resurrection of Christ. Therefore, he attempts to attack our minds, trying to convince us that the battle is lost and that we are

defeated. Satan is a liar. He is the Father of liars. We
have already won!

Up to this point, we have spoken a lot about
spiritual authority, and I want you to realize spiritual authority is something other than what you
work for. It is something that you inherit with your
salvation package. It is very similar to being born
into wealth when children are born into a wealthy
family; they do not have to work for it because of
their last name. By birth, they become joint heirs
immediately. This is the same with you and I in the
Kingdom of God. We are joint heirs!

In Genesis, chapter one, the Bible illustrates that
whatever God said was manifested because He is
the supreme authority. God gave that authority to
Adam.

> ¹⁹And out of the ground the LORD
> God formed every beast of the field,
> and every fowl of the air; and brought
> them unto Adam to see what he would
> call them: and whatsoever Adam called
> every living creature, that was the name
> thereof.
>
> Genesis 2:19 KJV

Because of the authority Adam received from
Father God, his words had authority in the earth.
Adam named the entire animal kingdom and pos-

sibly the oceanic kingdom by using his authority. When someone in authority walks into a room and begins to speak in a low tone or high volume, they get everyone's attention. That happens because the person carries that level of authority. One of the most outstanding examples is a judge in a courtroom. Everyone stands when he enters the courtroom because the judge's authority is recognized. He has the delegated authority over everyone in that courtroom. He received this authority from the county or the state government based on his qualifications to carry that authority.

> 23 And when he was come into the temple, the chief priests and the elders of the people came unto him as he was teaching, and said, By what authority doest thou these things? and who gave thee this authority? 24 And Jesus answered and said unto them, I also will ask you one thing, which if ye tell me, I in likewise will tell you by what authority I do these things.
>
> Matthew 21:23-24 KJV

We all agree that Jesus was the son of man and the son of God. One of the things He did in His earthly ministry was to set the standard for us to reach through His actions and teachings. As you read Matthew 21:23 - 24, notice that Jesus took the keys of authority from Satan. He went to Hell, took the keys, and gave us back those keys of authority. When we become born again, we become spiritually new in Christ Jesus. We must get the revelation that the spiritual world has authority over the earthly world. We must move on a spiritual level of authority that we have never done before. The religious elders of Jesus' day saw that He was not like them. Through Jesus, God gives us the spiritual ranking and the authority to operate supernaturally on earth. You might say, "How could I have any ranking. I have not been ordained or called to the ministry at this point". My question to you is simple: "Are you a believer?". If you answer yes, you already have the spiritual authority to operate as king and priest on earth.

Today's church must stop having church and become the church! Jesus died on the cross. He did not stop there. He did not just go to heaven. He went to Hades [HELL] and took the keys of death, Hell, and the grave from Satan. I am sure you have heard the phrase in the scripture, "Oh death where is your sting and O grave where is your victory?". Dear friends, there is a remnant army that God raised. He is not waiting for a lukewarm church to get in position. His remnant army is taking its authority on the earth. His army understands the kingdom's assignment on earth and is pursuing prophetic destinies. As you read this book, God is saying, "Stop waiting by the pool of Bethesda for someone to put you inside of your purpose/pool. No one is coming to help you because everything has already been done for you. Get up and take your authority; speak to things and call things into existence". That is what people do who understand their authority. The earth is mature and advanced and has left much of the church behind. That should not be the case. The Bible declares that "The ***kingdoms*** of this ***world*** are ***become*** the ***kingdoms*** of ***our Lord***, and of ***his Christ***" (Rev. 11:15); They will become such as we begin to take our rightful place of authority on the earth. Let us ask ourselves these two questions from Matthew 21.

- Question #1 - By what **authority** do you do these things?

  ○ Answer: God our Father

- Question #2 - Who gave you this **authority**.

  ○ Answer: God our Father.

⁶ And He raised us up together with
Him and made us sit down together
[giving us joint seating with Him] in
the heavenly sphere [by virtue of our
being] in Christ Jesus (the Messiah,
the Anointed One).

Ephesians 2:6 AMP

A person who carries himself in his position of
spiritual authority in this season must take their
seat of authority. Like Deborah, the judge of Israel,
she was a person of great authority and was ranked
as a judge over her nation. The scripture above is
a prophetic word to those mature in Christ Jesus.
God is saying to you: "Take your seat. I have already
raised you up, but you must be seated in your proper place to download what I am saying and doing in
your life". For you see, taking your seat means many
things, but most of all, it means I am in authority and
ready for marching orders. The Lord says "many
are in authority, but the authority was not given to
them from the heavenly realm". In this time and
day that we are living in, it is dangerous to be in
a place of authority without heaven's protection.
"However, know that I have raised you up. I say
again to you, take your seat of authority. You are on
the blueprint of heaven. The blueprint from heaven

comes with the backing of my word with my army of angels to assist you". THUS SAITH THE LORD!

During the Word of Faith movement, we were repeatedly taught about the believers' authority and who we are in Christ Jesus; now we understand why as we look back. The Holy Spirit was trying to equip the body of Christ with the understanding of our ranking and authority on the earth. During the last sixty to seventy years of movements in the body of Christ (the healing movement, the tent crusades of the 50s and 60s, the 70s with the Jesus movement, the pastoral and the Word of Faith movement, and the charismatic renewal) we lost sight of understanding spiritual rankings in the body of Christ. We are all brothers and sisters in Christ Jesus, but at the same time, we are still the army of the Lord. Every army has rank, order, and protocols in place. Ranking needs to be understood in our times because everything is watered down. It is also essential to recognize commitment, consecration, and levels of dedication. When a person commits to becoming a disciple, they become a follower of Christ. Jesus calls for disciples. Disciples are disciplined to follow Christ and are willing to pick up their cross and follow Him. And through weeks, months, and years of walking in obedience to the cause of Christ, a disciple will receive promotions [Psalms 75:6]. Spiritual rankings are genuine in the body of Christ. If there were no promotions, there would be no need for ranking.

New Covenant Spiritual Rankings

²⁷ Now you [collectively] are Christ's body, and individually [you are] members of it [each with his own special purpose and function]. ²⁸ So God has appointed *and* placed in the church [for His own use]: first apostles [chosen by Christ], second prophets [those who foretell the future, those who speak a new message from God to the people], third teachers, then those who work miracles, then those with the gifts of healings, the helpers, the administrators, and speakers in *various* kinds of [unknown] tongues.

1 Corinthians 12:27-28 AMP

I could write an entire book on these two verses. There is so much to say and to see in these two verses. First, I want to say that we have to understand what the Lord said to me years ago: "I do not have a church; I have an army!". With the help of the Holy Ghost, that has become a revelation to me. The other thing that is a revelation to me is the protocol of the kingdom. Yes, we are all brothers and sisters in Christ Jesus on one level, but when it is time to move out and do the works of Christ, there is a rank and order. I can break it down using 1 Corinthians 12:27. Paul defines the body of Christ as having many members. Then, by the Spirit of the Lord, Paul reveals what I define as Spiritual Ranking. Using the King James version, Paul says God has set in the church first Apostles and then secondarily Prophets. I love how the Amplified Bible brings it out here. The great apostle Paul says God has appointed first apostles and second prophets. We can break it down to terms of our jobs, politics, and business because there is an order and a chain of command.

I am very interested in the books of 1st and 2nd Corinthians because they define where the body of Christ is in the Church is today. In 1 Corinthians, the Apostle Paul had to address a very immature church. In 1 Corinthian 3:1 Paul said, "**And I, brethren, could not speak unto you as unto spiritual, but as unto carnal, *even* as unto babes in Christ.**" The Church is unspiritual when believers are spoon-fed. In this New Testament dispensation, we must walk out of our authority on earth and become spiritual giants. We should not rely on gimmicks and props to get people's attention. The Church is not a place for thirty-five-minute motivational speeches. When you walk in your authority and the power of God, you do not need a prop. The tangible presence of God speaks for itself through yielded vessels. God uses those who lay before Him weeping between the porch and the altar, crying out "less of me and more of You".

It is a big difference between 1 Corinthians 3 and 2 Corinthians 3. In 2 Corinthians 3, the body of Christ is mature and in a more significant place of authority and spiritual ranking. In 2 Corinthians 3:16, Paul tells us that when one turns to the Lord, the veil is taken away, and in 2 Corinthians 3:17, he expresses that "**Where the Spirit of the Lord is there is liberty**". Therefore, when we take our seats of authority in the spirit realm, the Holy Ghost begins to talk to us in-depth about spiritual things.

In 2 Corinthians 3:18, Paul talks about going from glory to glory. Praise God! Glory to God! The contrast is seen between 1 Corinthians 3 and 2 Corinthians 3. Some people in Christ Jesus do not know their authority and do not understand spiritual ranking. The great Apostle Paul explains that he cannot even converse with them. Let us continually search our hearts and ward off conversations with the demonic spirits of today that create the lukewarm church mentality.

> [8] The centurion answered and said, Lord, I am not worthy that thou shouldest come under my roof: but

speak the word only, and my servant
shall be healed. [9] For I am a man under authority, having soldiers under me:
and I say to this man, Go, and he goeth;
and to another, Come, and he cometh;
and to my servant, Do this, and he
doeth it. [10] When Jesus heard it, he mar-
velled, and said to them that followed,
Verily I say unto you, I have not found
so great faith, no, not in Israel.
                         Matthew 8:8-10 KJV

Matthew presents a fascinating story about authority and spiritual ranking. The centurion had
heard about Jesus before he met him. Jesus was going from city to city, demonstrating signs, wonders,
and miracles. People had heard about Jesus in many
places. In those days, there were no TVs or cable
or any media communication; they heard of the
amazing things Jesus did. Before meeting the centurion, Jesus had just come down from the mountain,
and many people had followed him. After that, he
healed a man that was a leper. The authority we
move into often speaks before we get to a place, and
people will hear about you before they see who you
are. That is a critical dimension of authority.

When the centurion started talking to Jesus, he
got His attention immediately with his first statement: **"I am a man in authority"**. As straightfor-

ward a statement as that is, I find it fascinating in today's society, especially in Christian leadership. People want to be in authority as pastors, bishops, apostles, or chief apostles, but they have no structure or protocol showing any submission to any form of authority. On the other hand, they want to be over everyone else. God's Kingdom does not work like that. We must respect structured protocol, recognizing who is in submission, who is in covenant relationship, and who are the counselors: the people of wisdom in our lives. The centurion shows Jesus that he understands that two kinds of people submit to authority: soldiers and servants. It would be best to have both types of people in your life when you are in authority. You need soldiers to go to battle: people who are willing to take a stand for the cause without question and sacrifice. You also need servants. When we use the word servant, we are not talking about enslaved people; we are talking about people connected to you and your cause for Christ. People willing to serve you and the cause of Christ that you represent. The Bible says Jesus marveled at the centurion's statement, **"I am a man under authority, having soldiers under me: and I say to this man, Go, and he goeth; and to another, Come, and he cometh; and to my servant, Do this, and he doeth it".**

One of the things I love about the word authority is that it attaches itself to the word protocol,

especially in the Kingdom of God. When we gen-
uinely become kingdom-minded people, these two
words, protocol, and authority, bring us to places
of maturity and authentic discipleship. Over time,
true discipleship will get you into sonship. We need
to begin to see ourselves as centurion soldiers in
the army of the Lord, recognizing our authority and
walking in our authority on the earth. That is so
important as we mature in our authority as sons of
God in this day and time we are living in. The whole
world is waiting for the sons of God to mature and
come into our sonship. It is time for us to stop
tiptoeing around the earth. We must embrace the
boldness of the Holy Ghost and walk the earth as
sons of God who joint heirs with our Lord Christ
Jesus.

Listen to the heart of this centurion soldier as he
approached Jesus boldly but humbly. He said, **"I am
a man in authority and a man under authority"**.
Many in the body of Christ need to get rid of this
passive attitude and the tiptoeing in the spirit and
begin to pray, "Father grant us boldness". The word
of God tells us in the book of Proverbs that the
righteous are as bold as a lion.

> [1] Let every soul be subject unto the
> higher powers. For there is no power
> but of God: the powers that be are or-
> dained of God. [2] Whosoever therefore

resisteth the power, resisteth the ordi-
nance of God: and they that resist shall
receive to themselves damnation. [3] For
rulers are not a terror to good works,
but to the evil. Wilt thou then not be
afraid of the power? do that which is
good, and thou shalt have praise of the
same: [4] For he is the minister of God to
thee for good.

                              Romans 13:1-4 KJV

Who's Really In Charge

The first thing I want to point out is this; Romans chapter 13 challenges believers to recognize all earthly authorities just like we recognize
the Church's spiritual authorities. As kingdom citizens, we cannot separate the two. No saved person
would respond like this, "I am going to do what I
want to do". If they do, eventually, they will pay
the consequences. Romans chapter 13 challenges
believers to become subject to all in authority.
Wherever you see the word powers in chapter 13,
that word is, as we have discussed, authority figures
(Police Officers, Politicians, First Responders, etc.).
  Verse One says, "**Let every soul be subject to
the powers and authority figures; there's no
power or authority figure but that which is of**

God." This is an example of a person who decides to go to school to become a police officer. The individual is willing to serve the community and swears an oath to protect and serve. The oath taken by swearing is very similar to making a covenant agreement.

At the end of verse one, Paul wrote, **"All authority or powers are ordained of God."** God has set aside the law, a legal system on earth, to govern right and wrong. That is understood because the word of God, the Bible, is the laws and regulations we must learn to obey. That is why it is devastating when a government official, county, or state official breaks the law because they have sworn to keep it.

Verse two is challenging because it says, **"If I resist the authority in charge, I am resisting God."** It says, **"I received to my self damnation."** A synonymous term for damnation is judgment. For example, let us say it is 2:00 am and you are on your way home. You come to a red light and you drive through the red light. There is no police officer around. As believers, we understand that we are supposed to obey the laws of the land. If you do not follow the law, even though you did not get stopped by a police officer and avoided a ticket, God will judge you for not stopping at that red light at 2:00 am. As kingdom citizens, we have a right to set an example on earth. I know what you say:

"Perfect these officials, these policemen, and these politicians".

Verse four tells us that when people make that oath to serve, they become the minister or servant of the Lord on the earth to establish law on the earth. All must obey them. When we do not follow them, we are not obeying the authority delegated to them and the rank they have received as delegated officials.

A Repeat of the Book of Judges

25 In those days there was no king in Israel: every man did that which was right in his own eyes.

Judges 21:25 KJV

As we close out this chapter on spiritual ranking and authority, I want to look at where I see today's Church. My question is, "Are we repeating the acts of the Judges?". The Book of Judges symbolizes the authority figures in Romans 13. They were like civil officials when Israel had no king, so God gave them Judges to help govern the people of God. Like governmental or civil officials, many Judges had flaws, like Samson and Gideon, but God still used them and gave them the authority to execute His will during their time. The first three Judges were Othniel,

Ehud, and Deborah. The following three judges were Gideon, Jephthah, and Samson. Out of all six of these judges, Deborah was the *only one with a flawless character*. We need to put a prophetic pen to this to say that in these last days, **Deborah's company has been rising**. Many women of God will walk in spiritual authority and carry a spiritual ranking that will identify that the Lord is with them. To all the women of God, be encouraged to read Deborah's life story. It is very encouraging. We all must understand that in this end time, there is a corporate anointing for men and women of God to work together like Deborah and Barak. Please keep in mind that these judges had the spiritual authority of that era. Everyone in Israel looked to them for wisdom, understanding, and proper decisions.

The Book of Judges 21:25 breaks down the human nature of all human beings. When there is no authority in place, everything falls apart. I would encourage anyone in leadership in the Church to establish the authority figure. Establish who is in charge and a chain of command (A level of ranking) so everyone involved understands the protocol established. The kingdom way is an example of order. Before the judges were established as leaders, it was obvious that Moses was in charge of the people of God during their eras. After the death of Moses,

God made it clear that Joshua was in charge as the leader and the authority figure.

The Book of Judges 2:10 tells us something exciting. It says, **"After the death of Joshua there rose another generation; they knew not the Lord. And that generation began to go in their own direction and establish their own way."**. The unique thing I love about Joshua is that he had excellent leadership training as Moses' successor. That is what made him a great leader. Great leaders must have an example to become a great leader. Become an Elijah to an Elisha. When you look at the five out of the six Judges, not including Deborah, they have no good example of spiritual leadership. All before them had authority, but all had flaws. So often in the body of Christ, we repeat the weaknesses of the Judges in the Book of Judges. We have a lot of people in authority. These people can lead but they need to be mentored appropriately. Yes. We have authority figures who are anointed, gifted, and ranked, but they do not possess the character and integrity to maintain the office they say God has called them to.

Spiritual Authority & Ranking Stories to Study:

- Moses, Miram & Aaron - Numbers 12

- Moses & Aaron - Exodus 32

- David & the Amalekite - 2 Samuel 1

- Acts 19

5

HISTORICAL, NATURAL, & SPIRITUAL BATTLES

THE HISTORY OF NATURAL & SPIRITUAL BATTLES

1 Chronicles 12:1
Now these are they that came to David to Ziklag, while he yet kept himself close because of Saul the son of Kish: and they were among the mighty men, helpers of the war.

[1] When thou goest out to battle against thine enemies, and seest horses, and chariots, and a people more than thou, be not afraid of them: for the Lord thy God is with thee, which brought thee up out of the land of Egypt. [2] And it shall be, when ye are come nigh unto the battle, that the priest shall approach and speak unto the people, [3] And shall say unto them, Hear, O Israel, ye approach this day unto battle against your enemies: let not your hearts faint, fear not, and do not tremble, neither be ye terrified because of them; [4] For the Lord your God is he that goeth with you, to fight for you against your enemies, to save you.

Deuteronomy 20:1-4 KJV

The book of Deuteronomy is written to a new and very young army. I like to call them the NEXT and the NOW generation. It is a historical manual filled with Apostolic directives from their leader: Moses. We need to elaborate on this amazing man of God! Even today, Moses is still greatly admired for his profound leadership. Moses was a true general who commanded and led the army of God's people to their place of promise. As we look at these historical, natural, and spiritual battles, we will see one general after another; some made good decisions while others made terrible decisions. I like to say everybody needs a Moses, someone who is connected to God and has the blueprint of heaven in their heart. Everyone should be in a relationship with a strong, bold leader who is dedicated to helping others reach their place of destiny and purpose. It is appropriate right now to stop and ask you, "Do you have a Moses in your life? Do you have someone who is properly connected or are you a one-person army?". I am just allowing you to think about this!

> **3** And shall say unto them, Hear, O Israel, ye approach this day unto battle against your enemies: let not your hearts faint, fear not, and do not tremble, neither be ye terrified because of them;
>
> Deuteronomy 20:3 KJV

History Is Important

Yes, history is essential; this chapter will read several accounts of spiritual and actual natural, historical battles. We will discuss both victories and defeats. I used to say that no army goes to battle without its generals. No army goes to battle without a person with a plan. Well, let me add a third thing; no army goes to battle without understanding the history of fighting. I do not know if you ever thought about it like this, but the Bible has thousands of historical battles. The Word of God is full of true stories about battles fought. As the Army of the Lord, we can gain a lot of natural and spiritual strategies on what to do and what not to do. For example, "You need not fight this battle" is a ubiquitous statement that believers can live by no matter what they are going through. Embrace the revelation and the understanding that you do not need to fight any battle by yourself.

In Deuteronomy chapter 20, Moses explained to the next generation, the Joshua generation, that the Lord was with them. Remember that some of the young generation were alive simultaneously with their parents from the previous generation. The older generation completely missed what God had for them because they did not understand God's vision for their lives. The young generation made history and started a new chapter for generations. It is essential that in every generation and every season of our lives, we must ask, "Am I here to follow the history of the past generation or to learn from their experiences?". The answer should be yes; you exist to create a historical movement. God called you to be a trailblazer, a pioneer, an Apostolic, and a Prophetic Endtime Soldier of the Cross of Christ.

A Famous Quote
History matters, it matters rather we tell the truth about what happened centuries ago and it matters where do we tell the truth about more recent history. It matters because if we can't we will never be able to face the present, guaranteeing that our future will be doomed.
Robert Jensen

I can appreciate those words, "History Matters"! He says in this quote that we will never be able to face the present situation and circumstances without our history. I agree! When I am void of the truth about my history, I lose the tenacity and determination to move forward because I lack a clear picture. Right here, I want to ask my readers to do something special for themselves and essential for their future. I want you to write down your spiritual history, the good and the bad. Look that over and pray about it to get the wisdom to move forward. This will help you have more successes than defeats in your spiritual walk through life.

A Spiritual Battle – Gideon And His Humble ARMY!

> [5] So he brought down the people unto the water: and the Lord said unto Gideon, Everyone that lappeth of the water with his tongue, as a dog lappeth, him shalt thou set by himself; likewise, every one that boweth down upon his knees to drink. [6] And the number of them that lapped, putting their hand to their mouth, were three hundred men: but all the rest of the people bowed down upon their knees to drink water. [7] And the Lord said unto Gideon, By the three hundred men that lapped will I save you, and deliver the Midianites into thine hand: and let all the other people go every man unto his place.
>
> Judges 7:5-7 KJV

Wow! This story takes me personally back to my boot camp experience. I know you are thinking, "what do you mean?". Well, from the time you step into your new home in Uncle Sam's Army, he's trying to change your mindset. One of the highest honors of your squad is to become the team leader. You want to become one of the top four soldiers that lead in marching. Just imagine that team leader or top four of the squadron marching directly behind the team leader. So, out of the fifty or sixty guys in your squadron, every day, soldiers try to prove to their drill instructors that they are the "biggest and baddest" in the group. No one is trying to be humble! No one wants to get on their knees and lap water like a dog! So now our brother Gideon says to himself, "I got 33,000 soldiers. I am ready to fight. I got an army and the Lord God is with us. It is time to go! Time to do this!". God stops him and tells him, "you have too many with you".

We must remember that we do not need any natural forces in a spiritual battle. We need to get in oneness and agreement with heaven. I would dare even say that some people may look at a huge church today with 8,000 plus members. Right away, we think that is a great movement and a powerful church. It appears more powerful than the little storefront church with four cars in the parking lot on Sunday morning. Many may never say anything, but some develop inner judgmental thoughts about that little church as they go to their church of 8000 members. The reality is that those four cars in the parking lot with seven to eight persons could represent consecrated people who are on fire for God, and sitting under an open heaven!

Remember what God said to the prophet in the book of Samuel; He does not look at the outward appearance of things. He looks at the heart. I know it is hard for many of you to believe that a Church with ten to twelve members can make any impact. The word we need to hear and understand is *agreement*. If any two or three come together in the name of JESUS, they become a force to be reckoned with on earth. Gideon's army is an excellent example, as it went from 33,000 to 10,000. It was a fantastic classic spiritual battle. God wants to use us to defeat His enemy. God took control of the army because the leader, Gideon, had postured his heart, (as seen in past encounters) to hear from God. In most Bible stories, commanding officers and generals' armies in many battles end up in defeat because of the pride of their hearts. They do not possess hearts of humility like Gideon!

We all know the story of Gideon from childhood Bible study in Sunday school lessons. We learned how God wins the battle for him not by many but by few. Victory came Not by 33,000, not by 10,000, but by 300! Paul told the Roman Church, "if God be for us who can be against us" (Romans 8:31). I pray in Jesus's name that we all get revelation as we digest this story into our spirits. I like the title, "Gideons

Humble Army". The title says it all because whoever heard of a humble army.

A Natural Battle: The Civil War – The Bat-
tle At The Potomac

Let us look at a natural battle that offers a great
history lesson - the battle at the Potomac. The
Potomac was a river in a critical location. It was
considered the Mason-Dixon line of the Civil
War in Montgomery County. The commanding
officer's name that is most memorable at the Potomac is General McClellan. President Lincoln
put him in charge of the Union Army at the Potomac. He was known for his great job preparing
his troops, training, and drilling. History tells us
that McClellan also helped establish the state of
West Virginia by taking his army to the battle. You
see, General McClellan and President Lincoln
clashed because of McClellan's leadership style.
He was very hesitant to go to war. I want you to
understand my point; if the southern army of the
Confederates can cross the Potomac, they can
create a lot of chaos for the Union army because
it brings them close to the capital of Washington,
DC. History tells us that several Potomac River
crossings caused much confusion. However, on
every account, the Union Army drove them back
from Washington, DC.

As I stated earlier, General McClellan was great at preparing for battle but was always over-cautious when it came time to go to war. Wow, It reminds me of the Church today. Yes, we can stay behind the four walls and have Church all day, but do not ask us to go outside and do anything. God needs believers to enter into strategic victories against their enemies. If you study the history of the Civil War, you will see that Abraham Lincoln frequented the telegraph office. He stayed on top of what was happening with his generals daily through messages from the telegraph office. President Abraham Lincoln tried to take over at one point because General McClellan was often slow to move forward in battle. At one point, McClellan had over 100,000 troops and was still asking Washington, DC, to send him more troops, horses, and military equipment. All students of Civil War history know that the Confederate army was usually much smaller and less equipped than the Union army. General McClellan had a massive army, but he would fight. Wow! That sounds like many saints and churches today. They are full of the word of God, revelation, and power of God, in the name of Jesus, with a host of angels, but we do not go to battle in the hedges and the highways in our communities. We do not go to battle in the seven mountains of society. For example, in education, we let the government tell us what kind of books children will read to frame their minds.

The goal is to make them think God created an Adam and a Steve and not an Adam and an Eve.

I could write a book about the Battle of the Potomac and the different events during the Civil War. The Potomac War can help us learn a lesson about kingdom life. We see that the enemy convinced General McClellan that his army was insignificant and incapable of winning the war. Let me give you an example: at one point, the Confederate Army generals circled McClellan's massive army with what they called Quaker cannon guns. They pointed them toward the Union Army, saying it was over. When the Union army saw the Quaker guns everywhere, the Confederates appeared well equipped, but the Quaker guns were only big log trees cut out to look like giant cannon guns. From a distance, no one could tell it was just a big tree log propped up in the air like a cannon. General McClellan panicked and became very fearful and hesitant. Eventually, Abraham Lincoln had to replace him with someone else.

Ask yourself, "What is your Potomac fear? What thoughts have the enemy put in your mind that have caused you to be unwilling to move forward, share the word of God, or speak to your situations? What prevents you from speaking to your mountains?". Remember what the great Apostle Paul said, "If God be for us, who can be against us?".

A Spiritual Battle: The Battle of Mount Gilboa

The battle of Mount Gilboa is a battle on many fronts. It was a battle in which the people's King, Saul, lost his life and his sons. This includes my favorite Old Covenant person, Prince Jonathan, who was David's covenant brother. Jonathan had an excellent heart for David and God's people, but this story is about his father's heart and how it led him, Saul, to lose his life in battle.

There are several things wrong with King Saul's reign. Most of the time, King Saul was going in the wrong direction. For example, when the ark of the covenant was lost, he never pursued the presence of God. Saul never went after the ark during the entire time of his reign as king. Even worse, he tried to kill one of his own: David. He wanted the life of the man who fought many battles for him. Saul recognized David for slaying Goliath. It was a great victory for the entire army of Israel. During another battle, Saul could not win against the Phillistines because he sought counsel from a familiar spirit instead of the presence of God. Wow! This is an excellent lesson for all of us to take note of and learn from. Many people in the Church are unable to figure out why they cannot win their battles against Satan. The devil is a defeated foe, yet most saints live in defeat.

¹ And it came to pass in those days, that the Philistines gathered their armies together for warfare, to fight with Israel. And Achish said unto David, Know thou assuredly, that thou shalt go out with me to battle, thou and thy men. ² And David said to Achish, Surely thou shalt know what thy servant can do. And Achish said to David, Therefore will I make thee keeper of mine head for ever ³ Now Samuel was dead, and all Israel had lamented him, and buried him in Ramah, even in his own city. And Saul had put away those that had familiar spirits, and the wizards, out of the land. ⁴ And the Philistines gathered themselves together, and came and pitched in Shunem: and Saul gathered all Israel together, and they pitched in Gilboa. ⁵ And when Saul saw the host of the Philistines, he was afraid, and his heart greatly trembled. ⁶ And when Saul enquired of the Lord, the Lord answered him not, neither by dreams, nor by Urim, nor by prophets. ⁷ Then said Saul unto his servants, Seek me a woman that hath a familiar spirit, that I may go to her, and enquire of her. And his

servants said to him, Behold, there is
a woman that hath a familiar spirit at
Endor.

1 Samuel 28:1-7 KJV

If we study the history of Israel's army and the
Philistine army, we will find out that the Philistine
army was much bigger than Saul's army. That did
not matter! If God sanctioned the battle, He would
fight it for His people. Do not forget that we do
not have to fight our battles. He will fight for us!
The spiritual lesson to learn is this: never go to war
with an evil heart, or you will end up in a place
like Gilboa. King Saul lost everything because he
considered his help his enemy!

God the Father had them put this story in the
Bible for a life-learning lesson. Like I said, there are
many things that King Saul did wrong, but the thing
that got heaven's attention more than anything was
his visit to the witch. In verse seven, it says he
inquired of a witch for direction to a victory. There
is something we need to investigate: what was it that
King Saul was supposed to do? He always depend-
ed on the prophet Samuel's direction. As king, he
didn't know the voice of God, nor did he know the
heart of God for himself. Remember, Samuel had
just died! Saul did not act like a general. Generals
normally strategize with what they have and make
it work. King Saul panicked like a coward! If he

had followed the protocol of that day, he would have contacted the priest and the prophet and then waited for instructions from the Lord. There is a protocol, even today, if you are waiting to hear from the Lord. When you are in a battle, you cannot panic and know what the word of God says. Do not be troubled by the size of the situation arrayed against you. The battle is not yours, but the battle is the Lord's.

We will close this section by understanding prophetically that the type of Saul's ruling and reigning season is over. Because there are still many Sauls, there will always be a religious order among us. However, understand this by the Holy Ghost; the House of Saul is getting weaker and weaker and the House of David is getting stronger and stronger. The two verses below give us a better prophetic view of where the Church is and where it is going. The Saul type of leadership with the wrong heart and motives is either dead or dying. The book of Revelation says it best to one of the churches in Asia Minor, "I have something against you". This is for all those who have a form of godliness but are denying the power. Saul was king, but he never really became the king; he never took on his rightful authority. Remember, he never pursued the presence of God, the Ark of the Covenant, and he never stopped chasing his son-in-law, David, because he was jealous of him. I want to point out

something significant about this Saul spirit.
When Saul went to battle with clear instructions
to get rid of everything and everyone, he com-
promised his assignment. That will preach! He
went to war, but he did not finish the job. As
a result, the prophet told him, "The Lord has
rejected you!". I know this is challenging to your
heart, but I want it to be. We must examine our
hearts and become more obedient to the Lord's
assignment.

> **6** So Saul died, and his three sons, and
> his armourbearer, and all his men,
> that same day together. **7** And when
> the men of Israel that were on the
> other side of the valley, and they that
> were on the other side Jordan, saw
> that the men of Israel fled, and that
> Saul and his sons were dead, they
> forsook the cities, and fled; and the
> Philistines came and dwelt in them.
> 1 Chronicles 10:6-7 KJV

Wow! The Philistines came and dwelt in their
cities, in their towns, in their states, and over their
nations! That is the reality of the world we live in
now: a spirit of compromise corrupted the society
of that day. Even now, we see it destroying our
communities today. Despite this, a David company

is rising, ready for battle, and saying, "Is there not a cause?".

A Natural Battle: The Crusaders & the Great Schism of 1054

Now, my friend, this is a fascinating story. Let me start by talking about The Crusaders. Yes, we have all watched movies like Knightfall and other historical dramatic movies like Knights of the Roundtable. My wife and I have watched it 15 to 20 times. I started watching it first, then I introduced it to her and she got hooked on the whole crusader concept. The knight in shining armor fought for a cause rather than life or death. However, the cause became confusing, and the assignment often needed clarification. I am sure many people believed the Crusaders were devout in their Christian faith and commitment to God. As you go back and study the life of the Crusaders, you will see that they were fighting battles like the Apostle Paul when his name was Saul. He thought he had a Godly cause. Many Christians today do not even understand nor embrace revelation on so many things. They seek to take a stand with no foundation to stand on.

3 Beloved, when I gave all diligence to write unto you of the common salvation, it was needful for me to write unto you, and exhort you that ye should earnestly contend for the faith which was once delivered unto the saints. **4** For there are certain men crept in unawares, who were before of old ordained to this condemnation, ungodly men, turning the grace of our God into lasciviousness, and denying the only Lord God, and our Lord Jesus Christ. **5** I will therefore put you in remembrance, though ye once knew this, how that the Lord, having saved the people out of the land of Egypt, afterward destroyed them that believed not.

Jude 1:3-5 KJV

The Great Schism Then

The Crusaders, alongside the Pope of Rome and the Catholic Church fought Greek Orthodox leadership of that day. This occurred at their headquarters in Constantinople. It became religion and idol worship on a whole new level. The conflict goes as far back as 190 AD when a Bishop of Rome wanted to excommunicate a Church Leader in Asia Minor. The fallout was on the day they celebrated Easter. There were countless other disagreements. The Western Catholic Church spoke and wrote in Latin, while the Eastern Greek Church spoke and wrote in Greek. This caused conflicting interpretations. The great schism was simply a lot of disagreements over interpretation. There was great debate about what should and should not be. For example, they debated questions like, "Should men marry or not marry?". It became a significant issue between the Catholic and the Greek Orthodox churches. We can see where that is at today. I do not even have time to discuss who made the right decision. Could you think about it? Now, down through the years, there have been several disagreements regarding doctrinal do's and don'ts and the interpretation of scriptures. How much authority did the Pope have against the church leadership of the Greek Orthodox Church?

The Great Schism of 1054 led to the separation of the Christian churches; the eastern and western branches broke apart into the Catholic and the Greek Orthodox. It is incredible how disagreements can create such an upheaval. We see this throughout the history of the early Church era. These two branches tried to come together in the

1960s during the Vatican Council and again in 1979, but very little progress has been made in hundreds of years. In reality, religious wars can be more conflicting than natural wars.

The next step in this whole thing is the New World Order system. The one world religious order will manage the entire new world order system. You see, friend, the spirit of religion, tradition, and doctrine has led to much fallout in humanity. I have not even touched the iceberg of this topic of the great schism in the early Church scandals in wars. Please be provoked now and research it for yourself. Study it. Many of my ministry peers today follow traditional ways of doing things from these two early churches. The religious order has no foundational premises in the early Church of the Book of Acts.

Before the Crusades that started in 1094, the Crusader's assignment was to fight the Muslims and to take back and maintain the Holy Land of Jerusalem. They had battles in the 11th, 12th, and 13th centuries. These were known as religious wars between Muslims and Christians. I know most of us get our understanding from the movies we watch, but my friend, these were brutal battles. If you go back to Constantine and move forward a couple of centuries, you find a constant warring within the ranks of the Christian faith over doctrine and many other things.

A Famous Quote
Know thyself, know thy enemy. A thousand battles, a thousand victories.

Sun Tzu

I encourage you to read up on this whole pe-
riod of the medieval dark ages. It is pretty fascinating. It is religion at its best! Do not get me
wrong, the Crusaders followed a religious order and
system. Times were very confusing, but their dedication and commitment to Christ, in many cases,
was something to be admired. We often see it run
parallel with our Christian faith. Devout Jews, Muslims, and countless other religions are faiths that
are far from the truth in doctrine, but their hearts
are very sincere, and that is what we see in many of
The Crusaders. Thank God for Martin Luther, who
came along years later and declared, "The just shall
live by faith". That propelled many believers to take
a stand for God during that day. It persuaded them
to not be so caught up in religion, idols, statues, and
human-designed ideas that are not God conceived
from the throne room of heaven. History tells us
that the Crusades started in 1095 and had nine significant campaigns.

Anyone who has ever read about the Crusades in
the Holy Land in either academic or popular litera-
ture has heard about the well-known slogan of the

Crusaders, from the time of the First Crusade on-
wards: '**Deus vult!** '(God wills it!). Now, as bold as
that may sound, I just kept emphasizing the courage
of the Crusaders—many of the battles they went
into were not the will of God. I know we love the
movies Knights, The Mighty Crusaders, and all the
pageantry. However, much of it was not the will
of God! To my fellow co-laborers in the gospel,
let us ensure what we are doing is not man's will
but God's will. The Apostle Paul said it best in the
book of Galatians, O foolish Galatians, who hath
bewitched you, having begun in the spirit, now you
follow after the flesh (Galatians 3:1). I find the life
of The Crusaders very similar to many that preach
and teach the gospel today. The devotion is there,
but the religious system they are in is out of order!

> **14** And profited in the Jews' religion
> above many my equals in mine own na-
> tion, being more exceedingly zealous of
> the traditions of my fathers.
>
> Galatians 1:14 KJV

Before Saul became the most excellent writer of
the New Testament, he had the baton passed on
to him by the traditional fathers in the religious
order. History tells us that he took that to another
level and started killing Christians because he felt
he was doing the right thing by upholding the tra-

ditions and doctrines of his day. During the Great Schism, there were three major religions: the Muslim faith, the Catholic faith, and Judaism. History shows us that the Christian faith was not only warring against the Muslims, but they started fighting amongst themselves over doctrine and tradition.

So, what have we learned from this great schism of 1054? I am unsure because there are many silent wars in 2024 in the body of Christ. We have our schisms going on today. There are silent wars on cultural, age, and gender differences. Today, these silent wars lead to bigger fights over doctrinal differences. As in 1054, we abandoned our assignment as the Church to go into all the world and preach the gospel of Jesus Christ. I want to admonish all believers and Church leaders to abandon the call of the Antichrist spirit, which brings division in the body of Christ, and instead fight for the unity of the faith. Examine yourself to see whether you are in the faith, and consider the Apostle Paul who is the greatest among all of us in the New Testament. The world tells us he was zealous for the wrong cause. Help me, Jesus, and help us, Jesus!

The Spiritual Battle: Deborah and Barak, Two Types of Leadership

The book of Judges gives us two different types of leadership. We see examples for us to follow and not follow as we look at the life of Deborah and Barak. Let us backtrack and look at history before Deborah, the fourth judge in the Book of Judges. Before we dive into our spiritual lesson from Deborah's life story, let us look at the book of Deuteronomy. This book represents a new generation getting new marching orders from their commanding general: Moses. I also encourage you to go back and research the book of Deuteronomy. It is a fascinating book for the body of Christ today. It shows you the heart of God. As much as God loves His people, He will leave them behind if they do not obey. As we discuss the life of Barak, we will see just that. Because of the disobedience of the Moses generation, God chose to raise another generation that would obey. Many times in life, we find ourselves in bad battles or spiritual warfare battles that we keep losing. We must inquire of our past to see if we have been disobedient somewhere. That disobedience could have opened the door to continue losing these battles against the enemy. Remember, the enemy is already defeated.

> [9] When your fathers tempted me, proved me, and saw my works forty years. [10] Wherefore I was grieved with that generation, and said, They do alway err in their heart; and they have not known my ways. [11] So I sware in

my wrath, They shall not enter into
my rest.) **12** Take heed, brethren, lest
there be in any of you an evil heart of
unbelief, in departing from the living
God. **13** But exhort one another daily,
while it is called To day; lest any of
you be hardened through the deceit-
fulness of sin. **14** For we are made par-
takers of Christ if we hold the beginning of our confidence steadfast unto
the end; **15** While it is said, To day if
ye will hear his voice, harden not your
hearts, as in the provocation.

Hebrews 3:9-15 KJV

Hebrews chapters three and four speak directly to the Moses generation: a generation that
represents much of what we see in the body of
Christ today. It is comprised of people who do
not understand their relationship with God and
His high calling on their lives to be obedient.
Many people who know me know I often quote
this phrase, "No army goes to battle without its
generals". There is a statement in the Book of
Judges Chapter 4, verse 1, "the children of Israel
again did evil in the sight of the Lord". This is
repeated over and over in the book of Judges.
This simply means they were disobedient!

The book of Deuteronomy is a book that prepares the next generation to enter into their new season. That generation is the Joshua generation. They obeyed and entered the land of promise because they obeyed God's voice and His appointed leadership. Let us pick up the story in the Book of Judges. The Judges' era is an exciting time. There were 15 recorded judges in the old covenant. We will discuss only some of them. However, in chapter three, we see the first Judge, Othniel, who freed God's people from eight years of bondage. He reigned as a Judge for 40 years and brought great peace to the people of God. The second Judge was Ehud. During his reign, the Israelites killed over 10,000 soldiers in a battle that conquered Moab. Moab became subject to Israel for eighty years until Ehud died. Many of these battles were spiritual battles that these judges fought in. They were vastly outnumbered. Of course, they were spiritual battles because only the Lord Jehovah Nissi could have won these battles for them. The third Judge was Shamgar. The account indicates that he fought one recorded battle and slayed 600 Philistines.

Now, let us give attention to the fourth judge. The study about this judge is fascinating because we are talking about a woman. At that time, women were not highly respected or used in any capacity. However, God decided to raise up a woman by the name of Deborah. We all know the story about how she sat under a palm tree as a judge for the people of God during her day. Deborah wore many hats. She was a prophetess, wife, mother, and judge. The position that made her most prominent was being a *military strategist*. Let us understand that God is using women like never before. Deborah was a forerunner for women. Think about it; she was a wife to her husband, a mother to her children, and a prophetess before the Lord God. Deborah was a judge, which means she was both a political and a spiritual leader.

Historically, whenever a judge died in Israel, people fell back into idolatry and sought after other gods. There was war at the gates. The Canaanites controlled the highways, causing the people to be afraid to travel the standard routes. The people of God's villages were devastated, resulting in moral decay.

> [6] In the days of Shamgar the son of Anath, in the days of Jael, the highways were unoccupied, and the travellers walked through byways. [7] The inhabitants of the villages ceased, they ceased in Israel, until that I Deborah arose, that I arose a mother in Israel.
>
> Judges 5:6-7 KJV

Deborah became a mother in Zion. God had already spoken to her to tell Barak to take the lead in the battle. I encourage you to go back and read it in the fourth chapter. Barak said something and did what many leaders would do today. He altered the plan of God. God had explicitly told Deborah to tell Barak to take the lead and take his army out first. On the contrary, he responded, you go first, and I will follow you. That was not what God said. We have to learn as leaders in the body of Christ that God does not need us to alter His commands; He needs us to obey His commands. So, the moral of this spiritual battle is to **follow every word of God**. When the blueprint comes from heaven through your leadership, keep the plan the same. History shows us this in many battles and the life of many generals. Barak had strategic plans, and he chose to alter them. I love that Deborah did not hesitate; she just said "I will go first" and she went as a great military strategist who won the battle. This is seen when she proclaims "And I Deborah rose a mother of Zion" (Judges 5:7).

A Natural Battle: The Battle at Midway

Here is another example of a natural battle in which we can gain spiritual understanding and wisdom from. It will help us as we face our own enemy one on one. Now, the Battle of Midway shows us an enemy thinking he can defeat a much more powerful foe or, should I say, army than themselves. If you think about it, the Japanese commanding officers and generals were crazy. Why do you say that? First of all, they were the smallest ones in the fight. They went out and started many battles against bigger foes. Let us look at it from a historical standpoint. Japan went to war against other small Asian countries, like themselves, and they defeated them. Their sole purpose was to acquire the rich materials of these countries to help sustain their country. Japan could not produce iron and many other products to build the necessary military force and weapons. As a tiny island nation, they did not have all the natural things to care for their people.

As they were conquering the other countries, around 1937, they decided to pursue and invade China once again. Now, the Japanese commanders had outstanding strategies. As big as China was, it could have had a better army than the Japanese. In terms of land, China is twenty-five times bigger than Japan. However, they were still being defeated by Japan. While invading China, they reached the point where they had consumed about 1/3 of China's land. In your own time, study the whole battle. Amazingly, this little country overtook this giant country like they did. For the sake of time, let me get to my point. As Japan continued to conquer China, they realized they would need more supplies, especially oil. Eighty percent of China's oil came from the USA at that time. At the same time, the USA was getting very alarmed by Japan trying to conquer all of these Asian countries, so the U.S. declared an embargo and shut off its oil supply to Japan; this is one of the reasons why Japan began to pursue a fight with the USA. As in all spiritual battles, you must become strategic to become the victor.

It is good to know your history. Most people in the U.S. may think the Empreor of Japan just woke up one morning and decided to attack America for no reason. When Japan attacked Pearl Harbor, it was a vicious attack. We all know the story. Japan had over 350 attack airplanes and devastated that island's naval base in Hawaii. It is fascinating that history shows us that the Japanese believed the United States would not fight back. Study history books. You will see it! That is exactly how the enemy is. He does not think you would have any fight left after his attack!

So after the Japanese attacked Pearl Harbor six months later, about 1000 miles away from there was another U.S. island called Midway. The Japanese decided to capture this small island called Midway. They believed they could use it as a guard post if the United States attacked them. It could be like a command center they could set up at Midway, and if the United States were attacking them with aircraft carriers or battleships, they could easily detect it. The rest is an extended military story of how the USA protected Midway from the Japanese taking it over. To make it brief, the USA defeated the Japanese at Midway because they had higher radio frequency technology, and their enemy, the Japanese, could not find their aircraft carriers. Wow! The Japanese could not detect those giant aircraft carriers in the ocean because they had outdated radio frequencies. Long story short, the U.S. won the battle and conquered Japan from then on, moving forward in the war.

My closing remarks and thoughts are that the USA could defeat a strategic enemy because they had higher frequency in radar equipment than the Japanese. Our frequency as believers is much higher than the devil's frequency. You can win every battle, big or small, in Jesus' name.

A Spiritual Battle: The Joshua Generation of Strategies

It is fitting to close out this book by analyzing the Joshua generation because that is who we are today. We are not like our forefathers, Moses' generation, who had God's promises right before them, but they chose to stay in their camp. God was taking them to their promised land that flows with milk and honey. However, they wanted to stay in their camp. We can

glean many spiritual life lessons from the generation of Moses. The one that stands out to me is that
they were more concerned with what they needed
right now than God's prophetic future for their life.
Years before they left Egypt, God had already spoken to their forefathers about their prophetic destiny. Unfortunately, they never got there! The first
strategic thing that happens with the Joshua generation is not on the battlefield but in their minds.
you see the words command or commanded three
times in the verses below. Just like in Uncle Sam's
military army, no matter which branch you join, the
first endeavor is to shift the way you think. The goal
is to turn you into his true soldier! There is a clarion
call to this End-time remnant army that the Lord is
raising. There is a commanding anointing, and this
comes from true Apostolic and Prophetic voices.
They could no longer move to the cadence of a
Moses-type flow. They had to shift to a new form
of leadership: *The Joshua Anointing.*

Verse ten shows that a fundamental strategy must
be implemented as the Holy Spirit moves today.
Notice that Joshua commands his leadership to
move throughout the host of the people, which was
millions of people.
He told the people that their days of wandering
in the wilderness were over and they are in a new
season now! The same is the case for you! You must
prepare yourself to go in!

⁹ Have not I commanded thee? Be
strong and of a good courage; be not
afraid, neither be thou dismayed: for
the Lord thy God is with thee whither-
soever thou goest. ¹⁰ Then Joshua commanded the officers of the people, saying, ¹¹ Pass through the host, and command the people, saying, Prepare you
victuals; for within three days ye shall
pass over this Jordan, to go in to possess the land, which the Lord your God
giveth you to possess it.

Joshua 1:9-11 KJV

The army that God is raising up now is an End-
time army. They have the spirit of the Joshua generation on them. They are not the ones to talk about
it, but they are ready to go and get it. It is simple,
my friend; that is my theological discourse of this
Joshua generation. They *Just Do It* like NIKE! As
tragic and devastating as the pandemic was, God
was still speaking to us through that. What do you
mean by that? He allowed us to be put out of the
Church, and we still have not interpreted our assignment. God wanted us to stop having Church
and be the Church! Yes! There is a shift from being
Church-minded. It is time to abort the Moses mentality, so we can become more Kingdom-minded.

The people who understand their assignment are to be territorial. They must go in and possess the land at all cost! They must become owners, not borrowers and not renters!

> [11] Put on the whole armor of God, that ye may be able to stand against the wiles of the devil. [12] For we wrestle not against flesh and blood, but against principalities, against powers, against the rulers of the darkness of this world, against spiritual wickedness in high places.
>
> Ephesians 6:11-12 KJV

Let us summarize some revelations from the Joshua generation's experience. They strategically moved with their leader, Joshua, to possess the land. You find them in Kadish Barner. One of the first things that Joshua did was send in spies to the promised land. Joshua's use of spies was called getting intel. Every great strategic army and general knows they need intel. It would help to lay out what you will do and how you will attack your enemy. You must have heard this story many times about Rahab, the harlot, and the spies. Our spies are our intercessors, our worshippers, and the prophetic anointing that resides in our services that produce prophetic seers. We must learn to acquire the intel that will enable us to develop the right strategies as we move forward into kingdom ministry. Church leaders today must know wherever their ministry is set up, the enemy around them has developed methods to stop them from succeeding. They have acquired intel on you, your life, your ministry, and your family. They know where and when to attack.

Create A Strategic Sound

> 2 And when the day of Pentecost was fully come, they were all with one accord in one place. 3 And suddenly there came a sound from heaven as of a rushing mighty wind, and it filled all the house where they were sitting
>
> Acts 2:2-3 KJV

About a mile past the Jordan River, the Joshua Generation's first assignment was to conquer the city of Jericho. History tells us that Jericho was a tremendously large place with massive walls, approximately 430,000 square feet in mass, 30 feet high, surrounding the entire city. There was no way to walk into that city. You had to get through the massive walls and the gate. We know how Joshua and the people from his generation were assigned to walk around the city countless times for several days. Please remember that Joshua and Moses had already fought several battles in the wilderness. He went into hand-to-hand combat with weapons against their enemies and defeated countless other tribes. When they crossed the Jordan River, his army was ready to fight but God shifted the strategy. They did not have to fight physically. They were told to create a sound. Joshua's army took the ram's horn and the shofar and made a sound. Let me rephrase; they made the right sound!

One of our most essential strategies today is our praise that worship's our God. I want you to understand that when you open your mouth as a kingdom citizen, you sound a war cry in the realm of the spirit. I want you to think about this; on the day of Pentecost, they came together in the upper room, and in that atmosphere of prayer, praise, and worship, they summoned heaven with their sound. As a result, heaven brought a sound to the earth. I am sure you have heard of many great singers who can steal and capture an entire audience of thousands and thousands of people with the gift of their voice. This is all because of one person's natural ability to sing and capture the heart of many. When you and I praise and worship, we do not just create a natural sound. Instead, we break through the barrier from earth to heaven and shift things in the eternal realm. It does not matter how good you sound. Glory to God! You can make a joyful noise. I want you to get

into your spirit the sound from heaven that hit
the earth on Pentecost, which shifted the world
as we know it and brought about a great move
of God that is still being spoken about today. It
was called the day of Pentecost, the outpouring
of the Holy Spirit, as promised in the book of Joel
2:28. It all began with the sound created in the
upper room. That sound summoned heaven to
make a sound in the earth. My God! Somebody
give God praise! That is powerful! Think about it;
you have that same ability. Can somebody take
a praise break and give God a shout of praise?
Glory to God!

> [5] On this side Jordan, in the land of
> Moab, began Moses to declare this law,
> saying, [6] The Lord our God spake unto
> us in Horeb, saying, Ye have dwelt long
> enough in this mount: [7] Turn you, and
> take your journey, and go to the mount
> of the Amorites, and unto all the places
> nigh thereunto, in the plain, in the hills,
> and in the vale, and in the south, and by
> the sea side, to the land of the Canaan-
> ites, and unto Lebanon, unto the great
> river, the river Euphrates. [8] Behold, I
> have set the land before you: go in and
> possess the land which the Lord sware
> unto your fathers, Abraham, Isaac, and

Jacob, to give unto them and to their
seed after them.

                              Deuteronomy 1:5-8 KJV

I could not think of a more fitting scripture to
finish this book. In verse five, Moses began to share
with Joshua's generation about God's plan for them
to go possess the land. Verse five says, "on this side
of Jordan". Moses was on the wilderness side of the
Jordan. Once Moses died, Joshua crossed over to
the other side of the Jordan River, and that is where
we understand Joshua chapter one takes place. It
is the place where God says to Joshua, "Moses, my
servant, is dead". Joshua then receives his military
command to go in and possess the land. The book
of Deuteronomy shows Moses giving instructions
to the Joshua generation. I will close out this book
by saying to the remnant army across the world's
nations, God is saying to you and me, His Endtime
Army to, "shift into kingdom partnership. It is time
for the body of Christ to possess the territory and
join the global move of the Holy Ghost to take
over".

Bible history tells us after Joshua crossed the
Jordan River and conquered Jericho, he ascended
from the valley to the high mountain region of Ai.
His army traveled for twenty miles and then did a
3000-foot climb to the High Peak of the mountain.
When they got up to the top, they defeated the

five kings that came to attack them. They also went on to defeat thirty-one other smaller enemy states. What is God saying to me and you as we close this book? He has given us the land. God has given us countless promises in the new covenant. We must be willing to fight to possess what He has for us.

> [8] Behold, I have set the land before you:
> go in and possess the land
>   Deuteronomy 1:8 KJV

The main difference between the Moses generation and the Joshua generation is that the Moses generation saw themselves as grasshoppers. Joshua's generation embraced their leader and the spirit of the leader. Joshua was a proven warrior. They went into the land and won every battle. You can do the same, my friend. Go in and possess the land that God has given you!

A Famous Quote
How well we survive this time of creative destruction, it really is, depends on each of us, on each of us fighting our individual battles of integrity, for integrity.
Maria Ressa